T. S. Eliot

THE LITERARY
AND SOCIAL
CRITICISM

ε

T. S. Eliot

THE LITERARY

AND SOCIAL

CRITICISM

by *Allen Austin*

INDIANA UNIVERSITY PRESS
BLOOMINGTON · LONDON   1971

Indiana University Humanities Series Number 68
Indiana University, Bloomington, Indiana

EDITOR: Hubert C. Heffner
ASSISTANT EDITOR: Rudolf B. Gottfried
ASSISTANT EDITOR: David H. Dickason

The Indiana University Humanities Series was
founded in 1939 for the publication of occasional
monographs by members of the faculty.

FOR

Susan, Wendy, and Sandra

Preface and Acknowledgments

Although Eliot's criticism seems to support the New Critical view that the poet and the poem are completely separate, his theory of poetry is essentially a theory of indirect personal expression. He sees the poem as a self-contained structure which suggests or implies through its pattern of action the emotions of the poet. His phrase "objective correlative," although referring to a situation or events or objects that are an adequate cause of the character's emotion, is an appropriate designation for his theory of expression—an objective structure which correlates with the poet's emotions.

The primary concern of this study is with Eliot's theory of poetry, his theory and practice of literary criticism, and his social and religious criticism. His criticism before 1928, at least that which has been most influential, concentrates on problems of esthetics, particularly on qualities of poetic style. After 1928 most of his criticism is social and religious. He becomes concerned not only with the "relation of poetry to the spiritual and social life of its time and of other times" (Preface [1928] to *The Sacred Wood* [1920]) but also with the nature of society, culture, and religion. In *After Strange Gods* (1934), *The Idea of a Christian Society* (1939), and *Notes towards the Definition of Culture* (1948) he attempts to analyze the moral implications of literature, the characteristics of the ideal Christian society, and the problems of culture, particularly as culture relates to religion.

* * *

I wish to acknowledge here the valuable help that I have received from Oscar Cargill and David Shusterman, both of whom took time out from their very busy schedules to assist me. Professor Cargill read and criticized the manuscript when it was in its early stages and again when it was near completion. Professor Shusterman read the manuscript a number of times and made many criticisms and editorial suggestions.

I should like to acknowledge also the courtesy of the following publishers who have given me permission to quote passages that are relevant to this study:

Harcourt Brace Jovanovich, Inc.—from "Tradition and the Individual Talent," "Hamlet," "The Metaphysical Poets," and "Shakespeare" in *Selected Essays,* by T. S. Eliot; from *The Idea of a Christian Society,* also by T. S. Eliot; and from Eliot's preface to *Anabasis,* by St. J. Perse

Harvard University Press—from *The Use of Poetry and the Use of Criticism,* by T. S. Eliot*

Faber and Faber—from *After Strange Gods,* by T. S. Eliot

I am further indebted to the editors of several journals who have permitted me to reproduce in the present volume parts of some articles of my own: "T. S. Eliot's Objective Correlative," in *University Review,* 26 (Dec. 1959), and "T. S. Eliot's Quandary," *University Review,* 27 (Dec. 1960); "T. S. Eliot's Theory of Dissociation," in *College English,* 23 (Jan. 1962); and "T. S. Eliot's Theory of Personal Expression," *PMLA,* 81 (June 1966).

* The foreign rights to these publications are held by Faber and Faber, who have also given me permission to quote the passages in question.

Contents

T. S. Eliot

THE LITERARY
AND SOCIAL
CRITICISM

THE CRITICAL STANDARD

Poetry and Impersonality

MUCH of twentieth-century criticism is preoccupied with combatting the individualism and impressionism of the Romantic Movement. The ethical criticism of Irving Babbitt, one of Eliot's teachers at Harvard, is concerned with establishing, in opposition to Rousseauism, an objective standard of behavior which transcends individual preferences. The main efforts of the New Critical Movement concentrate on formulating objective esthetic criteria that relate only to qualities in the work itself. Eliot's early criticism, which began in earnest about 1917, is also an attempt to establish objective criteria—an "impersonal" standard, "independent of temperament," opposed to both impressionistic and abstract criticism. Whatever reservations Eliot expresses about Arnold as a critic, he has been influenced by Arnold's conception of the main task of criticism as an attempt "to see the object as it really is," to judge literature by universal standards.

In "Tradition and the Individual Talent" (1919), Eliot proposes that we set up an ideal of literary value based on tradition, on a comparison of contemporary poets with poets of the past.[1] The order of world literature, the pattern of "existing monuments" which possess a degree of excellence, is the "something outside of the artist to which he owes allegiance" ("The Function of Criticism," *SE*, p.13). If the poet is to produce a new work of art, he must conform to this order, this tradition. At the same time, his work, if it is genuine art, alters the existing order so that the "proportions, values of each work of art toward the whole are readjusted." We should "not find it preposterous," Eliot continues, that the present alters our view of the past.

Like Arnold, Eliot believes that the critic should see literature as timeless: "It is part of his business to see literature steadily and to see it whole; and this is eminently to see it *not* as consecrated by time, but to see it beyond time; to see the best work of our time and the best work of twenty-five hundred years ago with the same eyes."[2] Although Eliot advises the critic to provide the reader with historical facts about the work—"its conditions, its setting, its genesis" (*SE*, p. 20)—he regards the relationship of the work to its own time as "documentary" and relatively unimportant. The work gains its significance by its portrayal "of truth permanent in human nature" (*SE*, p. 142).

One of Eliot's purposes in advancing the idea of tradition is to underplay the importance of the individual talent in relation to tradition. Eliot consistently stresses the importance of order and authority, of something outside the writer. At the time that he made the statement on tradition (1919), he apparently did not want his aims as a poet to be construed as a break with the past, as an attempt to establish the individual poet as an isolated poet. The idea of tradition later becomes in Eliot's thought a synonym for order and custom. In *After Strange Gods*, for example, he defines tradition as the "habitual actions, habits and customs" of people living in the same place, as contrasted to orthodoxy, which is an authority achieved by the exercise of "conscious intelligence."[3] But in "Tradition and the Individual Talent" his purpose is to advise the poet to be aware of tradition and to set up tradition (the order of world monuments) as a literary standard.

Eliot, however, makes no attempt to define the specific qualities of the tradition to which the poet owes allegiance. His impersonal standard is not, in fact, related to tradition but to the values inherent in the work itself: "it is not the 'greatness,' the intensity, of the emotions, the components, but the intensity of the artistic process, the pressure, so to speak, under which the fusion takes place, that counts. The episode of Paolo and Francesca employs a definite emotion, but the intensity of the poetry is something quite different from whatever intensity in the supposed experience it may give the impression of" (*SE*, p. 8).

In *The Achievement of T. S. Eliot* F. O. Matthiessen interprets "process" to mean form or craftsmanship: "With Arnold, in so far as you can make such a division, the emphasis is on substance rather than form. . . . With Eliot, the emphasis is on form."[4] Certainly, many passages in Eliot may lead one to make this interpretation. For example, in his introduction to Valéry's *Le Serpent* (1924), Eliot says, "not our feelings, but the pattern which we make of our feelings, is the centre of value."[5] And in "The Function of Criticism" (1923): "the dry technique implies, for those who have mastered it, all that the . . . [reader] thrills to; only that has been made into something precise, tractable, under control" (*SE*, p. 20).

Nevertheless, Eliot's standard is not primarily technical excellence. In the conclusion of "Tradition and the Individual Talent," he says that although a number of people appreciate technical excellence "very few know when there is an expression of *significant* emotion, emotion which has its life in the poem and not in the history of the poet" (*SE*, p. 11). In "The Perfect Critic," he maintains that the technical critic is limited in his approach, although such criticism "is of great importance within its limits" (*SW*, pp. 11–12).

The basis of Eliot's critical standard is the intensity of emotion in the poem.[6] The function of poetry "is not intellectual but emotional" (*SE*, p. 118); the poet attempts to "capture and put into literature an emotion."[7] Eliot's objection in "Tradition and the Individual Talent" to Wordsworth's theory of "emotion recollected in tranquillity" is to the explanation of how emotion gets into poetry, not to the emotional basis of the theory. Although Eliot calls the creative process an escape from emotion, he views emotion as the basis of poetry.

Wordsworth stresses the joy of the creative process; Eliot, the release from suffering, from personal and private agonies. The poet "is oppressed by a burden which he must bring to birth in order to obtain relief." During the creative process, he is motivated to write by his desire to express himself in words: "He is not concerned whether anybody else will ever listen to them or not, or whether anybody else will ever understand them if he does."[8] The poet's aim is to choose "whatever subject matter allows . . . [him] the most powerful and most secret release."[9] Eliot's description of the poet's feeling of release in completing the poem is similar to the familiar Romantic metaphors of birth or volcanic action: "a moment of exhaustion, of appeasement, of absolution, and of something very near annihilation, which is in itself indescribable" (*On Poetry and Poets*, p. 107).

Eliot defines the creative process as "depersonalization," which he illustrates with his analogy of the catalyst (*SE*, pp. 7–8): oxygen (emotions) and sulphur dioxide ("feelings" or images) mixed in the presence of a filament of platinum (the poet's mind) produce sulphurous acid (the art work). The central point of the analogy is the separation of the "man who suffers" from the mind of the poet. The process is impersonal because the poet does not express his personality directly, but concentrates on his medium, on the task of creating an impersonal structure.

Poetry as Indirect Personal Expression

Although the catalyst analogy presents the poet's mind (the "filament of platinum") as detached, the materials of the poem—"feelings" related to images, and "emotions" related to situations—are internal; and the poem is created by a process of "fusion," which occurs under intense pressure. The fusion depends on (1) the emotions of the "man who suffers," (2) the transforming power of the creative process, and (3) the fortunate critical moment—the "concentration" that produces the right combination of elements.

Whereas Wordsworth emphasizes the poet's spontaneous emotion, Eliot emphasizes the poet's fusion of experiences—the intensity of the pressure which fuses images and emotions. In spite of his insistence on the importance of intellect, Eliot subordinates conscious purpose to spontaneous creation. The intellect is involved in the trying out of technique[10] and in the "frightful toil" of revision (*SE*, p. 18), but the creative moment is an "unpredictable" crystallization. As in Wordsworth's concept of the creative process, the role of the intellect is confined to a time before or after the moment of creation. The catalyst analogy, in fact, emphasizes spontaneity or unconscious creation, the detached mind passively attending on the event (*SE*, p. 10), on the crystallization of the poem from "depths of feeling into which we cannot peer."

Eliot's concept of the poetic mind as a catalyst has similarities to the Romantic analogue of the lamp, discussed by M. H. Abrams in *The Mirror and the Lamp*. Both Eliot and the Romantics emphasize the qualities of the external (images and situations) as reflections of the internal (emotions and personal characteristics)—that is, the personal expression of the poet as opposed to the representation of the world in which the poet lives. The catalyst, however, does not become a part of the work, the mind of the poet remaining outside the "newly formed" art (*SE*, p. 7)—an idea which seems to support the theory of impersonality. The poet's mind, however, or the poet as poet, has no personality to express; only a medium in which to work. The personality of the man, at the time of creative activity, is separate from the mind of the poet. But after the poem has been completed, the pattern of the characters' actions (*SE,* p. 173) reveals the personality of the poet—which is, except for the time of creation, the same as the personality of the man.

Whatever the degree of "impersonality" of the creative process, the poem itself is personal, indirectly reflecting the personality behind it. "No artist," Eliot says, "produces great art by a deliberate attempt to express his personality. He expresses his personality indirectly through concentrating upon a task which is a task in the same sense as the making of an efficient engine or the turning of a jug or a table-leg" (*SE,* p. 96). The personality is extinguished in the poetic process, in the task to be done, but not in the work itself. Massinger "did not, out of his own personality, build a world of art, as Shakespeare and Marlowe and Jonson built" (*SE,* p. 192). "We often feel with Shakespeare, and now and then with his lesser contemporaries, that the dramatic action on the stage is the symbol and shadow of some more serious action in a world of feeling more real than ours."[11] Eliot cites the passage from *Macbeth,* "Tomorrow and tomorrow and tomorrow . . .," and comments, "Is not the perpetual shock and surprise of these hackneyed lines evidence that Shakespeare and Macbeth are uttering the words in unison, though perhaps with somewhat different meaning?" (*On Poetry and Poets,* p. 110).

The theory that the poet indirectly expresses his personality is associated in nineteenth-century criticism with the analogue of God the Creator, who remains invisible but immanent in the world he creates. Friedrich Schlegel applies the analogue to "objective poetry" ("everywhere the feeling of the author—even the innermost depths of his most intimate individuality—gleams through"), and John

Keble, to all poetry ("Poetry is the indirect expression . . . of some overpowering emotion").[12] Eliot, like the Romantics, cites Shakespeare as the most forceful example of the analogue: "The world of a great poetic dramatist is a world in which the creator is everywhere present, and everywhere hidden" (*On Poetry and Poets*, p. 112)—a statement referring not only to the dramatist's artistic imprint on the play, but also to the dramatist's expression of personality: "The whole of Shakespeare's work is *one* poem; and it is the poetry of it in this sense, not the poetry of isolated lines and passages or the poetry of the single figures which he created, that matters most. A man might, hypothetically, compose any number of fine passages or even of whole poems which would each give satisfaction, and yet not be a great poet, unless we felt them to be united by one significant, consistent, and developing personality" (*SE*, p. 179).

Poetic drama gives the pattern or undertone "of the personal emotion, the personal drama and struggle, which no biography, however full and intimate, could give us; which nothing can give us but our experience of the plays themselves" (*SE*, p. 180). Cyril Tourneur's *The Revenger's Tragedy*, for example, reveals a "highly sensitive adolescent" with an "intense and unique and horrible vision of life." The "objective equivalents" of Tourneur's "cynicism, . . . [his] loathing and disgust of humanity," are "characters practising the grossest vices; characters which seem merely to be spectres projected from the poet's inner world of nightmare, some horror beyond words" (*SE*, pp. 165–66). Eliot believes that Tourneur's emotion was so strong and unmanageable that Tourneur could not create characters who adequately represent it.

The essay on Tourneur involves two problems related to personality: the work as an expression of personality, and personality as a cause of value in the work's impersonal structure. Eliot's rejection of personality as a quality of the poet's mind (*SE*, p. 7) is a rejection of the belief that the personalities of man and poet, during the creative process, are unified; but Eliot does not deny that personality may be one of the sources of value. The value of the poet's external world is partially dependent on the genuineness of his inner life, which this world symbolizes: A "dramatic poet cannot create characters of the greatest intensity of life unless his personages, in their reciprocal actions and behaviour in their story, are somehow dramatizing, but in no obvious form, an action or struggle for harmony in the soul of the poet" (*SE*, pp. 172–73).

In an essay on Yeats (1940), Eliot explains what he means by personal and impersonal: "I have, in early essays, extolled what I called impersonality in art, and it may seem that, in giving as a reason for the superiority of Yeats's later work the greater expression of personality in it, I am contradicting myself." But the impersonality of the mature artist, as opposed to the impersonality of the craftsman, includes an intense expression of personality: the mature artist creates a "general symbol" which expresses the "particularity" of "intense and personal experience" (*On Poetry and Poets*, p. 229). Whereas Eliot's earlier statements on impersonality are concerned with the creative process, with the poet as a craftsman who probes "the abyss" of personal emotion, escaping his personality, the statement on Yeats is concerned with the relationship between the impersonal structure and the expression of the poet's personality. Eliot does not deny that the work of any poet may express personality, but contends that the work of the mature poet possesses "a greater expression of personality" and that this expression increases esthetic value.

Eliot's opposition to "biographical" criticism is not an opposition to the concept that poetry is personal expression, but to the concept that the "feeling, or emotion, or vision" of the poet is the same as the feeling, or emotion, or vision of the poem (*SW*, p. x). Eliot's frequently cited statement that "If we write about Middleton's plays we must write about Middleton's plays, and not about Middleton's personality" (*SE*, p. 140) does not reject the value of personality, but confesses that the personality of Middleton, who is the "most impersonal" of Elizabethan dramatists, cannot be discovered in his plays. Shakespeare or Jonson had a personal point of view, but "with Middleton we can establish no such relation" (*SE*, p. 141).

The reason that Eliot appears inconsistent in his theory is that he views the poet, whether lyric or dramatic, as both craftsman and expressionist, who concentrates on the task at hand and escapes his personality, but at the same time creates an impersonal structure which usually reflects, through the pattern of the characters' actions, his personality—a concept represented by the opposing metaphors of internal release (the birth of a burden) and external construction (the turning of a jug or a table leg). The poem itself is an autonomous world in which the poet, like the dramatist, is "everywhere present and everywhere hidden." Eliot combats the theory that the poem depends on the spontaneous expression of the poet's emotions rather than on the poet's power to fuse images ("feelings") and situations ("emotions"); but in Eliot's own theory the creative process is spontaneous, and the poem is indirectly expressive. The poem's impersonal structure has, of course, intrinsic value, but expression of the poet's personality creates additional value—at times, as in the work of Shakespeare, the most significant value.

The argument against Eliot's standard of personal expression is represented by contextualist theory. The argument of Wellek and Warren, for example, is that the poet's personal emotion is irrelevant to the value of the work. Although we may need biographical information to "explain a great many allusions or even words in an author's work,"[13] the author's personality or emotions should not influence our critical evaluation. The expression of personality in the poem is no more relevant to esthetic value than the author's sincerity or insincerity.

Eliot's theory agrees with at least one point of contextualist theory—that the poet's personality cannot give value to a work that itself lacks value. Personality can be expressed, of course, in bad works of art. But if the work possesses value, the reader's appreciation may be enriched by recognition of personal meaning. A critical evaluation can be made without reference to biography or personality, but recognition of the author's personality, based primarily on the pattern of the characters' actions, may increase appreciation as well as understanding of the work of art.[14]

Although appreciation of the poet's personality is esthetically valid, Eliot's statement that Shakespeare's personality is what "matters most" represents an extreme position. Biographical information may be a key to the basic meaning of a work, but personal expression is not a central standard of value. It can be, however, an enrichment of esthetic appreciation. For example, Milton's reference to his blindness in Samson's "O dark, dark amid the blaze of noon" is, as Douglas Bush says of *Lycidas*, "impersonal art charged with personal emotion"[15]—a statement paralleling Eliot's definition of the mature artist as one who creates a general symbol which expresses intense and personal experience.

The important point is that Eliot recognizes that the poem is an integral part of the poet. Eliot's interest in impersonality is, first of all, a concern with the poet's strategy, with the poet's concentration on his task rather than on his emotions; and secondly, a concern with impersonal art as a representation (a "general symbol") that possesses universal significance. But in spite of this concern, Eliot consistently shows interest in the "depth" of personal emotion and in the poet's personality, which stands behind the poem's objective structure.

The Art Emotion

Eliot agrees with Pater that the critic, in order to see truly, must refer the art object to his own emotions: "All we can hope to do, in the attempt to introduce some order into our preferences, is to clarify our reasons for finding pleasure in the poetry that we like" (*SE*, pp. 267–68). "If we are moved by a poem, it has meant something, perhaps something important, to us; if we are not moved, then it is, as poetry, meaningless."[16] "For the development of genuine taste, founded on genuine feeling, is inextricable from the development of the personality and character."[17]

The problem with which Eliot deals is the relationship between the individual response and objective literary value. If the individual response is related to temperament, then how can we say that the values of literature are objective? Eliot attempts to solve the problem by distinguishing between the ideal (objective literary value) and the reality (the individual response). What we try to do, Eliot says, is to transform the individual response into objective value, but the goal can never be fully achieved. We ought to respond to art as art, but our adventitious likes and dislikes constantly interfere.

Eliot establishes as the basis of his ideal of objective value an art emotion, "an experience different in kind from any experience not of art" (SE, p. 8).[18] What seems clear to Eliot is that the difference between art and the event portrayed by art must be absolute; otherwise we would respond to the event as we respond to it in actual life. But Eliot, as is clear in context, does not refer to an art emotion in the sense of an esthetic response to form. What he tries to account for is the difference between art and its materials. The distinction he makes is not, in fact, absolute: "Great variety is possible in the process of transmutation of emotion: the murder of Agamemnon, or the agony of Othello, gives an artistic effect apparently closer to a possible original than the scenes from Dante." Whether or not emotion is related to an actual experience, the art emotion is not the same as the actual emotion related to the experience; but it is different in degree, not in kind.

The differences between art and its materials depend on a "fusion of elements," on the transformation of situation by images. The reader's response to this transformation, as opposed to his response to the materials of art, is an art emotion: "a pure contemplation from which all the accidents of personal emotion are removed" (SW, pp. 14–15). Ideally, the individual's personal response will correspond

to the art emotion, which is impersonal because it is dependent on an objective structure: "The personal to one-
self [the reader] is fused and completed in the impersonal
and general, not extinguished, but enriched, expanded,
developed, and more itself by becoming more something
not itself."[19]

Eliot's attempt to solve the paradox of the subjective
response and objective value forms the basis of his essay on
the perfect critic—a critic who builds his personal impressions into "laws" (an idea of Rémy de Gourmont). The
weakness of Arthur Symons as a critic, Eliot says, is that he
presents his impressions without attempting to analyze
them or to transform them into general principles. Symons
is creative, rather than critical. Swinburne, on the other
hand, moves in "the direction of analysis and construction"
(SW, p. 5); and Aristotle provides an example of a critic
whose personal responses coincide with objective analysis.
Aristotle fulfills the role of the ideal critic, whose sensibility (individual response) and perceptions (of the art object)
are the same—a combination of appreciation and intellect.

The question is whether Eliot's principle—the objective
analysis of impressions—is an adequate account of the
critical act. If the critic begins with his impressions, rather
than the qualities of the work, his impressions, no matter
how much he analyzes them, will remain impressions. If
they become valid "laws," related to the work itself, then
the fact that they began as impressions is unimportant for
criticism. We should make a distinction between literary
experience (our response to a work) and literary criticism
(our commentary on a work, whether interpretative or
evaluative). We may want our experience as readers to correspond to our task as critics; but what is important for

criticism is not our response—our appreciation or lack of appreciation—but the validity of what we say about the work. There is no way to lead from response to criticism and still retain the pure qualities of the response. As soon as the critic begins to relate what the work means or what it is worth, he is giving intellectual reasons for his interpretation or judgment. The response to a work is experiential, whereas criticism of the work is conceptual. Aristotle does not present his feelings about the work, but attempts to analyze its qualities according to his standards of mimesis —to ascertain the depth and fullness of the poet's representation. A critic's criticism will no doubt be affected by his response, but the value of the criticism is dependent on the quality of critical penetration of the work, not on an analysis of the critic's response to it.

Eliot discusses the problem of literary criteria within the framework of his emotional theory, which includes the emotions of poet, work, and reader. Eliot assumes that all poets begin with their own emotions, which are transformed into an objective structure. The objective structure has its emotion, and the reader responds with his own emotion, evoked by the work. The value of the work is dependent on the intensity of the representation of the emotion and on the expression of the poet's own emotion, which is hidden behind the objective structure. Although Eliot shows great interest in the poet's emotion, saying at one point that it is the most significant esthetic quality, he is usually interested primarily in the emotional intensity of the work itself.

[II]

THE INTENSITY OF POETRY

Situation and Images

IN THE statement of his concept of poetic intensity in "Tradition and the Individual Talent," Eliot distinguishes between "emotion" and "feelings," illustrating his point with a passage from Tourneur:

In this passage (as is evident if it is taken in its context) there is a combination of positive and negative emotions: an intensely strong attraction toward beauty and an equally intense fascination by the ugliness which is contrasted with it and which destroys it. This balance of contrasted emotion is in the dramatic situation to which the speech is pertinent, but that situation alone is inadequate to it. This is, so to speak, the structural emotion, provided by the drama. But the whole effect, the dominant tone, is due to the fact that a number of floating feelings, having an affinity to this emotion by no means superficially evident, have combined with it to give us a new art emotion. [*SE*, pp. 9–10]

The structural emotion is dependent on the situation, and the floating feelings on images. The poet may create poetry "without the direct use of" emotions taken from actual life (*SE*, p. 8), as did Dante in his description (Canto XV, *Inferno*) of Brunetto Latini running to overtake his companions (he ran like those in Verona who run for the green cloth, and he seemed like one in the winner's, not the loser's place)—an image which may have been held in suspension in Dante's mind. Dante creates this image out of a "feeling" (toward Brunetto's running as compared with running for the green cloth) which may have had no direct relation to the situation in life, Dante's attitude toward Brunetto. But this lack of direct relationship applies only to the creative process, not to the artistic effect. For Eliot does two things in his discussion: he speculates about what happens in the process of creation and at the same time attempts to analyze the effect after the creation has been completed.

Eliot's concept of the creative process has some similarity to John Livingston Lowes's account (in *The Road to Xanadu*) of the process by which Coleridge created "Kubla Khan" and "The Rime of the Ancient Mariner." In *The Use of Poetry and the Use of Criticism* Eliot applies Lowes's analysis to poetic creation in general, saying that Coleridge undervalues the role of memory, a power which supplies the poet with images, and which is, in fact, a part of imagination as well as fancy:

And I should say that the mind of any poet would be magnetized in its own way, to select automatically, in his reading (from picture papers and cheap novels, indeed, as well as serious books, and least likely from works of an abstract nature, though even these are aliment for some poetic minds) the

material—an image, a phrase, a word—which may be of use
to him later. And this selection probably runs through the
whole of his sensitive life. There might be the experience of
a child of ten, a small boy peering through sea-water in a
rock-pool, and finding a sea-anemone for the first time: the
simple experience (not so simple, for an exceptional child, as it
looks) might lie dormant in his mind for twenty years, and
re-appear transformed in some verse-context charged with
great imaginative pressure. [pp. 78–79][1]

Although Eliot is careful to point out that creation involves conscious "critical toil," he believes that unconscious processes, the accumulation of experience which
results in "unpredictable crystallizations," are crucial: "The
development of experience is largely unconscious, subter-
ranean."[2]

Why, for all of us, out of all that we have heard, seen, felt, in
a lifetime, do certain images recur, charged with emotion,
rather than others? The song of one bird, the leap of one fish,
at a particular place and time, the scent of one flower, an old
woman on a German mountain path, six ruffians seen through
an open window playing cards at night at a small French rail-
way junction where there was a water-mill: such memories
may have symbolic value, but of what we cannot tell, for they
come to represent the depths of feeling into which we cannot
peer. [*UP*, p. 148]

After the poet has drawn on images held in suspension
in his mind, he achieves the artistic effect, the proper combination, when the image, though it does "not develop
simply out of what precedes," becomes a part of the whole.
The image is no longer "floating," but has an "affinity to
. . . [the] emotion by no means superficially evident." In
separating emotion and feelings Eliot attempts to account

for the creative process, not the artistic effect, which is dependent on an "affinity" expressed by the interaction of situation and images. The "feelings . . . have combined with it [the structural emotion] to give us a new art emotion."

Eliot stresses the idea that one of the ways in which poetry achieves intensity is through the embodiment of an emotion in a concrete object:

it is universally human to attach the strongest emotions to definite tokens. Only, while with the Russian the emotion dissolves in a mass of sensational detail, and while with Wordsworth the emotion is of the object and not of human life, with certain poets the emotion is definitely human, merely seizing the object in order to express itself. When Donne says:

> When my grave is broke up again . . .
> And he that digs it, spies
> A bracelet of bright-hair about the bone

the feeling and the material symbol preserve exactly their proper proportions. A poet of morbidly keen sensibilities but weak will might become absorbed in the hair to the exclusion of the original association which made it significant; a poet of imaginative or reflective power more than emotional power would endow the hair with ghostly or moralistic meaning. Donne sees the thing as it is.

When Wordsworth, however, fixes his attention upon: "The meanest flower that blows" his attitude is utterly different. His daffodil emphasizes the importance of the flower for its own sake, not because of association with passions specifically human.[3]

Eliot's attitude toward the objects of poetry is similar to that of the imagists, although Eliot expands their theory: "The aim of 'imagism,' " he says, "was to induce a peculiar concentration upon something visual, and to set in motion an expanding succession of concentric feelings."[4]

The poet, according to Eliot, may increase intensity by eliminating exposition or explanation, concentrating on a combination of images:

any obscurity of the poem [*Anabasis* by St.-J. Perse], on first readings, is due to the suppression of "links in the chain," of explanatory and connecting matter, and not to incoherence, or to the love of cryptogram. The justification of such abbreviation of method is that the sequence of images coincides and concentrates into one intense impression of barbaric civilization. The reader has to allow the images to fall into his memory successively without questioning the reasonableness of each at the moment; so that, at the end, a total effect is produced.

Such selection of a sequence of images and ideas has nothing chaotic about it. There is a logic of the imagination as well as a logic of concepts. People who do not appreciate poetry always find it difficult to distinguish between order and chaos in the arrangement of images; and even those who are capable of appreciating poetry cannot depend on first impressions. I was not convinced of Mr. Perse's imaginative order until I had read the poem five or six times.[5]

Although Eliot recognizes in his theory of poetry the importance of situation, he does not define poetry mimetically but linguistically, distinguishing poetry from prose on the basis of its greater emotional intensity, achieved not only by a fusion of images and situation (*SE*, p. 8) but also by an integration of thought and image (*SE*, pp. 246–47). In his essays on the Metaphysical poets and Andrew Marvell, he extolls the nondiscursive Image (the total integration of idea and sensation), defining the dissociation of sensibility which presumably occurred in the seventeenth century as partially a separation of idea and image. Eliot's distinction between poetry and prose follows closely the Romantic concept that the distinguishing quality of poetry is the nature of its images. This is why he can say in the essay on Marvell that "the perennial task of criticism" is to "bring the poet back to life" by squeezing "the drops of the essence of two or three poems" (*SE*, p. 251). He never develops the theory he sets forth in "Tradition and the Individual Talent," that poetry is an integration of situation and images. Sometimes, as in the essay on *Hamlet*, he stresses situation, but in most of his early criticism he is more concerned with images, with the objects of poetry to which "feelings" are attached.

The Objective Correlative

Most interpretations of the objective correlative define it as an image or series of images or a situation that expresses emotion—the emotion of the character in the poem or of the poet or both; for example, in Eliot's poem on Prufrock the image "measured out my life with coffee spoons" or the series of images relating to "half-deserted streets" or the entire situation in which Prufrock is involved is held to be an objective correlative that expresses Prufrock's feeling of futility and perhaps a similar emotion in the poet. In fact, however, these interpretations take Eliot's definition out of context and incorrectly regard the correlative itself as something that expresses emotion. The objective correlative refers, in Eliot's terms, to a "situation" or "set of objects" or "chain of events" that motivates the emotion of the character in the poem, an emotion which differs from the emotions of both poet and reader.

Thus, in *Hamlet* the objective correlative of Hamlet's despair is Gertrude's hasty marriage to Claudius, and the despair that Hamlet feels is *his* emotion, expressed by Hamlet, not by the objective correlative (his mother's behavior). The same point can be made by referring to the situation of bereavement—caused by the death of a friend or relative. Here, and in strictly common-sense terms, the objective correlative is the death of the friend, and the emotion is expressed by the individual who experiences the loss. In other words, the correlative is not the expression of grief but the cause of the emotion of grief. Although Eliot frequently shows interest in the problem of objectively expressing an emotion by means of images, the term objective correlative does not in itself refer to the expression of emotion but to the cause of emotion—to the situation or chain of events or set of objects that gives rise to the particular emotion felt by the character in the poem.[6]

In his essay on *Hamlet* Eliot notes that it is precisely the equivalence of the objective correlative to the emotions evoked that accounts for the "artistic inevitability" of the more successful tragedies and the insufficiency of the objective correlative that explains the failure of *Hamlet:*

The only way of expressing emotion in the form of art is by finding an "objective correlative"; in other words, a set of objects, a situation, a chain of events which shall be the formula of that *particular* emotion; such that when the external facts, which must terminate in sensory experience, are given, the emotion is immediately evoked. If you examine any of Shakespeare's more successful tragedies, you will find this exact equivalence; you will find that the state of mind of Lady Macbeth walking in her sleep has been communicated to you by a skilful accumulation of imagined sensory impressions; the words of Macbeth on hearing of his wife's death strike us as if, given the sequence of events, these words were automatically released by the last event in the series. The artistic "inevitability" lies in this complete adequacy of the external to the emotion; and this is precisely what is deficient in *Hamlet.* Hamlet (the man) is dominated by an emotion which is inexpressible, because it is in *excess* of the facts as they appear. And the supposed identity of Hamlet with his author is genuine to this point: that Hamlet's bafflement at the absence of objective equivalent to his feelings is a prolongation of the bafflement of his creator in the face of his artistic problem. Hamlet is up against the difficulty that his disgust is occasioned by his mother, but that his mother is not an adequate equivalent for it; his disgust envelops and exceeds her. It is thus a feeling which he cannot understand; he cannot objectify it, and it therefore remains to poison life and obstruct action. None of the possible actions can satisfy it; and nothing that Shakespeare can do with the plot can express Hamlet for him. And it must be noticed that the very nature of the *données* of the problem precludes objective equivalence. To have heightened the criminality of Gertrude would have been to provide the formula for a totally different emotion in Hamlet; it is just *because* her character is so negative and insignificant that she arouses in Hamlet the feeling which she is incapable of representing. [SE, pp. 124–25]

There are numerous interpretations of this definition as an image or a series of images which express emotion. For example, Grover Smith, Jr., in *T. S. Eliot's Poetry and Plays* (Chicago, 1956), interprets the term to mean a single image: "It [the poetry of *The Family Reunion*] is too symbolically concrete, too imagistic. Phrases like 'The unexpected crash of the iron cataract,' 'The bright colour fades,'

'the bird sits on the broken chimney' are good in themselves but are not closely relevant; they are 'objective correlatives' for emotion that an audience wants to see
justified in the plot" (p. 213).

The interpretations of F. O. Matthiessen and Eliseo
Vivas include situation as well as a series of images. Matthiessen says that *Samson Agonistes* provides Milton with
a dramatic situation which enables him to "externalize his
own emotions and thus give them universal stature." Later
Matthiessen refers to images: "A passage from 'Gerontion'
will furnish perhaps the best example of the kind of hard
precision with which Eliot's reliance upon 'a set of objects'
enables him to thread together the range of his associations." Matthiessen cites Eliot's phrase "the suggestiveness
is the aura around a bright clear center" (from the essay
on Marvell) and comments, "This necessity to concentrate
on something definite is exactly what Eliot means by his
repeated statement that the evocation of emotion by
means of complete, concrete objectification is the only
right way of expressing emotion in art." Eliseo Vivas's interpretation is similar: "The expression of the emotion or
emotions—for there is of course a whole complex of them
referred to throughout the poem—is achieved through the
presentation of these objects and situations; these are the
objective correlatives."[7]

But Eliot's whole essay is about the inadequacy of Hamlet's motive, "a motive which is more important than that
of revenge" and which has not been imposed "successfully
upon the 'intractable' material of the old play" (*SE*, pp.
122–23). Eliot's argument is that the crimes of Hamlet's
mother are not a sufficient motive for Hamlet's emotion:
"his disgust envelops and exceeds her." "To have height-

ened the criminality of Gertrude" would have motivated a "totally different emotion in Hamlet" (SE, p. 125). Hamlet's disgust is caused by something more than his mother's guilt; the weakness of the play, according to Eliot, is that Shakespeare does not provide this "something more," an adequate "objective correlative" to motivate the emotion in Hamlet. If Eliot were referring to images, then he would have criticized Hamlet for its inadequate imagery, its poor "sensory impressions." Although he says that the versification is variable, he makes no criticism of the imagery as an inadequate expression or "objectification" of emotion. Matthiessen, however, uses his interpretation of the objective correlative as a basis for criticizing the lack of concrete imagery in poetry. Although Matthiessen begins his essay (in *The Achievement of T. S. Eliot*) with a quotation from Arnold that the "eternal objects of poetry" are "human actions," he concludes that Donne and Campion are dramatic poets because their imagery is clear and visual, presenting a "sharp dramatic picture." This interpretation misses the point that Eliot's criticism of *Hamlet* is not of its lack of clarity and precision of imagery but of its lack of motivation.

It is true that according to my interpretation the phrase "a skilful accumulation of imagined sensory impressions" (referring to *Macbeth*) is puzzling. The term "skilful" implies that the images in *Macbeth* are successful, whereas those in *Hamlet* are not. However, the phrase "this exact equivalence" in Eliot's definition does not refer to the equivalence between Lady Macbeth's "state of mind" and the "sensory impressions," but to that between "a set of objects, a situation, a chain of events" and the "*particular* emotion." The situation, Eliot says, "must terminate in sensory experience." That is, the only way the situation can be expressed is through a series of images. The images in the sleep-walking scene are skilful because they refer convincingly to the cause of Lady Macbeth's emotion—her deep involvement in the murder of Duncan. Eliot's statement that Hamlet's emotion is "inexpressible" does not mean that Hamlet fails to express the emotion, but that Shakespeare fails to represent it convincingly, to provide adequate motivation.[8] The key to the meaning of the term is the cause or motive of emotion, the justification of emotion in the plot.

Although Matthiessen and Vivas include situation as well as images in their interpretations, they ignore situation as a cause of the character's emotion. They assume that the situation (or work) is an expression of the poet's emotion. Certainly, both Eliot's definition and the context of the definition seem to support this view. Not only does Eliot use the phrase "expressing emotion," he also argues that the basis of the "failure" of *Hamlet* is the inability of Shakespeare to find a situation which adequately represents his own emotion: "the bafflement" of Shakespeare "in the face of his artistic problem. . . . the buffoonery of an emotion which he cannot express in art. . . . we assume it [that is, Shakespeare's emotion] to be an experience which, in the manner indicated, exceeded the facts" (*SE*, pp. 125–26).

Nevertheless, the important emotion is that of the character, not that of the poet. Even if we assume that Eliot believes that Shakespeare's emotion is the same as that of Hamlet, Macbeth, and Lady Macbeth, we still have to conclude that Eliot's objective correlative refers to the character's emotion, because, as his examples indicate (Lady

Macbeth's "state of mind" in the sleep-walking scene and Macbeth's expression of emotion on hearing of his wife's death), Eliot is concentrating on the emotion *in* the play, not on the emotion of poet or reader. Matthiessen's and Vivas's assumption that the correlative is a situation which serves as a bridge between the poet's emotion and the reader is disproved by Eliot's examples and his central concern, the situation which motivates Hamlet.[9] If Eliot considered the correlative merely as a bridge, then the character, his situation, and his motivation would be irrelevant; the only important quality would be the situation which represents the emotion of the poet.

Eliot's failure to confine his consideration of the objective correlative to the motive of the character's emotion, his speculation about Shakespeare's personal emotion and situation, introduces confusion into the definition. Actually, throughout his discussion Eliot refers to two different types of correlative—one in life, the situation which is inadequate to Shakespeare's emotion, and one in art, the situation which is inadequate to Hamlet's emotion. According to Eliot, Shakespeare had some kind of experience, perhaps the reading of the *Apologie de Raimond Sebond* combined with some personal experience, which produced an emotion, disgust or horror, in excess of the situation; he was therefore unable to create an adequate objective correlative or motivation for Hamlet's emotion. He was unable to "intensify the world to his emotions" (*SE*, p. 126), to separate the "man who suffers" from the "mind which creates" (*SE*, p. 8).

The reason why Eliot would like to understand Shakespeare's personal experience and emotion is that they would help to explain the "failure" of *Hamlet*. If Eliot had

concerned himself only with Shakespeare's emotion, then
Matthiessen's and Vivas's interpretations would be valid.
But the introduction of the character's emotion and situation changes the whole problem, shifting it to the work itself. According to the concept of the objective correlative,
the only way of creating or representing emotion in the
poem, whether lyrical or dramatic, is by portraying a situation or set of objects or chain of events capable of motivating the character's emotion. The correlative is not related
to the poet's emotion, except as a part of the total work,
and it does not express, symbolize, or represent, but rather
causes, the character's emotion.

Another misconception, connected with the interpretation of the correlative as a bridge between the poet's emotion and the reader, is the belief that the correlative
arouses in the reader the emotion of the poet or the work.
Vivas is not sure that this is Eliot's meaning, but in his
analysis of the term he assumes this meaning. Joseph Ship-
ley's main objection to the term is that "Eliot confuses
expression of an emotion in the work with its arousal in
the receptor."[10] And R. W. Stallman asserts that the "objective correlative of the poet's original emotion . . . immediately evokes in the spectator the same emotion."[11]
Eliot, however, is consistent in his belief that the situation
created by the poet or the work as a whole cannot control
the response of the reader: "A poem may appear to mean
very different things to different readers, and all of these
meanings may be different from what the author thought
he meant" (On Poetry and Poets, p. 23). A crucial principle
in Eliot's poetic theory is that the poem has a life of its
own, related to but different from the emotions of both
poet and reader. The term "evoked" in the definition

means that the emotion of the character is brought forth, not that it arises in the audience. The audience recognizes Hamlet's or Macbeth's emotion, but does not necessarily experience that emotion. Shakespeare's failure, according to Eliot, is not his inability to make the audience feel Hamlet's emotion, but his inability to provide a situation capable of motivating an emotion which is convincing to the audience.

Eliot's belief that there was something wrong with Shakespeare's personal emotion, that it did not have an adequate correlative in life and thus hampered his creation of a work of art, is irrelevant to a consideration of the emotion in the work. If the cause of the emotion in the work is inadequate, then the correlative is inadequate; if there is no cause, then there is no correlative. For example, Coleridge's criticism of Iago's "motiveless malignity" can be legitimately interpreted as a criticism of the lack of an objective correlative for the malignity. Although the correlative involves images (the expression, the termination in "sensory experience"), its real basis is the motive or cause of the character's emotion.[12]

The insistence of W. K. Wimsatt, Jr., and M. C. Beardsley, in "The Affective Fallacy," on an actual cause of emotion is an insistence on an objective correlative in the sense in which Eliot uses the term. Wimsatt and Beardsley divide the "objects" of emotion into two kinds— "the literal reasons for human emotion, and those which by some kind of association suggest either the reasons or the resulting emotion—the thief, the enemy, or the insult that makes us angry, and the hornet that sounds and stings somewhat like ourselves when angry." The authors illustrate their point with an example from *Macbeth:* " 'Light

thickens and the crow makes wing to the rooky wood'
might be a line from a poem about nothing, but initially
owed much of its power, and we daresay still does, to the
fact that it is spoken by a tormented murderer who, as
night draws on, has sent his agents out to perform a further
'deed of dreadful note.' "[13] The image alone has no objective correlative; it is expression without cause, as Hamlet's
expression, according to Eliot, is expression without adequate cause. The objective correlative is provided by the
situation of a murderer instigating a further murder, and
thus the power of the image is increased, although the
image in itself is good.

It is ironic that a term which advances the idea of the
importance of motive has been primarily used to represent
the opposite idea, the importance of images as an expression of emotion, of texture as opposed to structure, or images as opposed to plot. The term has been widely used to
designate the objective representation of emotion because
it seemed to meet a need. Although the concept is central
to Romantic theory, being expressed at one time or another by almost every Romantic poet and critic, there had
been no single term to designate it. Furthermore, the term
provided ammunition in the battle against the Victorian
and Georgian poetry of statement and thus served the
cause of Imagism.

The concept of the objective correlative is an extension
of Eliot's statement in "Tradition and the Individual Talent" that the "art emotion" is dependent on an "affinity"
between feelings (images) and emotion (situation). Although Eliot concentrates, in his formulation of the objective correlative, on situation, he is in his critical practice

more interested in images than situation. In his theory, however, he provides for the primary importance of situation or motive.[14] According to this theory, intensity is dependent on both the dramatic situation and the images that are combined with it (*SE*, p. 8).

The Dissociation of Sensibility

Eliot's concept of the dissociation of sensibility is a modification of Coleridge's theory of imagination, Eliot viewing the integration of dissimilars in poetry as involving ideally an interaction between intellect (or wit) and emotion.

It [the difference between Donne and Tennyson or Browning] is something which had happened to the mind of England between the time of Donne or Lord Herbert of Cherbury and the time of Tennyson and Browning; it is the difference between the intellectual poet and the reflective poet. Tennyson and Browning are poets, and they think; but they do not feel their thought as immediately as the odour of a rose. A thought to Donne was an experience; it modified his sensibility. When a poet's mind is perfectly equipped for its work, it is constantly amalgamating disparate experience; the ordinary man's experience is chaotic, irregular, fragmentary. The latter falls in love, or reads Spinoza, and these two experiences have nothing to do with each other, or with the noise of the typewriter or the smell of cooking; in the mind of the poet these experiences are always forming new wholes.

We may express the difference by the following theory: The poets of the seventeenth century, the successors of the dramatists of the sixteenth, possessed a mechanism of sensibility which could devour any kind of experience. They are simple, artificial, difficult, or fantastic, as their predecessors were; no

less nor more than Dante, Guido Cavalcanti, Guinizelli, or
Cino. In the seventeenth century a dissociation of sensibility
set in, from which we have never recovered; and this dissociation, as is natural, was aggravated by the influence of the
two most powerful poets of the century, Milton and Dryden.
Each of these men performed certain poetic functions so mag-
nificently well that the magnitude of the effect concealed the
absence of others. The language went on and in some respects
improved; the best verse of Collins, Gray, Johnson, and even
Goldsmith satisfies some of our fastidious demands better than
that of Donne or Marvell or King. But while the language became more refined, the feeling became more crude. The feeling, the sensibility, expressed in the *Country Churchyard* (to
say nothing of Tennyson and Browning) is cruder than that in
the *Coy Mistress.*

The second effect of the influence of Milton and Dryden
followed from the first, and was therefore slow in manifestation.
The sentimental age began early in the eighteenth century, and
continued. The poets revolted against the ratiocinative, the
descriptive; they thought and felt by fits, unbalanced; they
reflected. In one or two passages of Shelley's *Triumph of Life,*
in the second *Hyperion,* there are traces of a struggle toward
unification of sensibility. But Keats and Shelley died, and
Tennyson and Browning ruminated. [*SE,* pp. 247–48]

The term "dissociation of sensibility" is generally interpreted as a split between images and ideas, which
presumably occurred in the seventeenth century. The explanation is that poems became either imagistic or abstract
or that the same poem presented images in one place and
ideas in another. This explanation, as far as it goes, is
valid; for Eliot's examples from Tennyson and Browning
are examples of abstract poetry, and Eliot asserts that the
Romantic poets "thought and felt [created images] by fits"

(*SE*, p. 248). The difficulty in Eliot's definition is not, as
F. W. Bateson maintains, in the term "felt," which has
been correctly interpreted by Basil Willey as "image" (a
combination of sensation and emotion).[15] The difficulty is
in the term "thought."

Eliot does not use "thought" in reference to the unified
sensibility in the ordinary sense of "meaning," of concepts
which may be judged as true or false. Eliot's theory is unrelated to Willey's thesis that the rise of science and ration-
alism brought about the belief that the images and myths
of poetry were no longer true and that therefore poetry
became either pleasant fictions (images) or abstract statements which attempted to conform to truth. The separation, in Willey's view, is between images ("phantasms")
and "truth" (ideas believed to be true). But Eliot is not concerned with this loss of belief in the truth of poems. He is
concerned rather with the loss of intellect, of "tough reasonableness," which is irrelevant to philosophical truth: "A
philosophical theory which has entered into poetry is established, for its truth or falsity in one sense ceases to
matter, and its truth in another sense is proved" (*SE*, p.
248). What Eliot regrets is the loss of "ratiocination" or
play of intellect combined with sensation-emotion (images), the substitution of reflection or rumination for
metaphysical wit. Whereas Willey concentrates on the
breakup of religious unity caused by the loss of belief in
the intuitive truths of religious myths, Eliot concentrates
on the breakup of the presumed integration of sensation,
emotion, and wit in metaphysical poetry.

The term "thought" in Eliot's definition refers to abstract
ideas in relation to the dissociated sensibility, but it refers
to wit or play of intellect in relation to the unified sensibil-

ity. That is, in Eliot's view, the "felt thought" of the Metaphysicals involves not only the integration of sensation and idea, the feeling of thought "as immediately as the odour of a rose" (*SE*, p. 247), but also a special kind of thought —a detached intellectuality combined with passion. Although Eliot maintains that an amalgamation of disparate experience is a characteristic of all poetry, he refers to a special amalgamation, which presumably the poets following the Metaphysicals lack—the infusion of intellectual experience, such as the reading of Spinoza, into emotional experience, such as falling in love. This concept of amalgamation is narrower than Coleridge's theory of the unity of opposites, and Eliot does not, in fact, maintain that all poetry possesses this particular type of amalgamation. Eliot's distinction is between the intellectual or metaphysical poets (including the Elizabethans and Jacobeans) and the witty (Neoclassical), the emotional (Romantic), and the reflective (Victorian) poets.

Eliot is not attempting, as Frank Kermode believes,[16] to establish a rationale for the nondiscursive image, but rather a rationale for wit combined with emotion. Eliot's argument is that wit dissociated from emotion causes the separation of ideas from images, the poet writing exclusively either from the "cerebral cortex" or from the heart. When he formulated his theory, Eliot, unlike Willey, was not concerned with defending religion and poetry—the truth-yielding image or intuitive way of knowing—against the encroachments of science. Nor did he, like T. E. Hulme, blame the presumed separation of ideas from images on the loss of religious belief. He was interested in establishing a poetic of metaphysical wit, in defending poetry which is both witty and emotional, the kind of poetry that he himself was writing. The concept of the integrated image is incidental to his defense of intellectual poetry. In Eliot's theory, the sensationalism of Rémy de Gourmont is subordinated to a metaphysical poetic.

The context of Eliot's definition clearly reveals this emphasis on the dissociation of wit and emotion. In the first place, Eliot is reviewing Herbert Grierson's *Metaphysical Lyrics and Poems of the Seventeenth Century* (Oxford, 1921), and he follows closely Grierson's idea of "passionate thinking," of the blend of "passion and thought, feeling and ratiocination." "Passionate thinking [Eliot's "felt thought"] is always apt to become metaphysical, probing and investigating the experience from which it takes its rise" (p. xvi). "With the peace of the Augustans the mood changed, and poetry, ceasing to be witty, became sentimental; but great poetry is always metaphysical, born of men's passionate thinking about life and love and death" (p. lviii).

In the second place, Eliot, citing Milton and Dryden as examples of dissociation, argues (in the Marvell essay) that these two poets exemplify the separate directions of poetry—wit and magniloquence or levity and loftiness, poetry becoming either witty or emotional, not a unity of both (*SE*, p. 252). Modern poets, Eliot adds, may be ironical or satirical but they "lack wit's internal equilibrium," or they may be "serious" but are "afraid of acquiring wit, lest they lose intensity" (*SE*, p. 263).

In addition to this dissociation of wit from emotion and of ideas from images, there is another dissociation, which interpretations of Eliot's term have usually ignored, that of language *from* sensibility, what Eliot calls the first effect of dissociation: "the language became more refined, the feeling [which Eliot here uses synonymously with "sensibility"] became more crude" (*SE*, p. 247). Racine and Baudelaire, who exemplify the unity of language and sensibility, are masters of diction and "the most curious explorers of the soul," whereas Milton and Dryden, also masters of diction, "triumph with a dazzling disregard of the soul." Thus, the poet's finding of the "verbal equivalent for states of mind and feeling" involves not only the "transmuting" of ideas into sensations, but also a deep interest in these states of mind, a sophisticated sensibility integrated with language (*SE*, pp. 248–49).

The dissociation of sensibility involves, then, a split between wit and emotion, ideas and images, and language and sensibility. But the dissociation with which Eliot is most concerned is that of wit and emotion, which is irrelevant to Willey's idea of truth or to W. K. Wimsatt's concept of the "grounds" for emotion. Wimsatt maintains that in the seventeenth century poetry retreated "into an area of feeling and emotion conceived as pure and prior to, or separate from, the objects of knowledge which had previously been considered their grounds."[17] Wimsatt's argument is that the loss of trust in the "meanings conveyed by poems" drove poetry into a pure emotionalism; thus, the rational grounds for emotion were lost. Eliot, however, is not defending the grounds for emotion; he is lamenting the loss of intellectual poetry, the amalgamation of intellectual and emotional experience. The intellectual experience which Eliot cites, the reading of Spinoza, is not the "grounds" for emotion, but a part of the representation of "states of mind and feeling," conveying "great variety and complexity." Intellectual experience, in Eliot's view, is a part of man's complete experience, including the "cerebral cortex" as well as the heart, "the nervous system, and the digestive tracts" (SE, p. 250).

Eliot's theory of the integration of wit and emotion has caused confusion because Eliot equates the combination of wit and seriousness with the reconciliation of opposite or discordant qualities, with Coleridge's idea of imagination. Such a stretching of the meanings of wit and emotion leaves ample space for thought and emotion, which have been variously interpreted as truth and emotion, as cognitive "grounds" and emotion, and, of course, as idea and image.

Eliot believes that all poetry is to some extent "witty": "a degree of heterogeneity of material compelled into unity by the operation of the poet's mind is omnipresent in poetry" (SE, p. 243). The best poetry "turns suddenly with that surprise which has been one of the most important means of poetic effect since Homer" (SE, p. 254). Eliot's concept is similar to I. A. Richards's distinction between poetry of inclusiveness (a high degree of heterogeneity in unity) and exclusiveness, except that Eliot concentrates on single lines or passages rather than whole poems. Eliot's praise of the Metaphysicals indicates not only his preference for a particular style of poetry (the integration of wit and emotion) but also his belief that intensity is dependent on "heterogeneity of material compelled into unity." Coleridge conceives of the reconciliation of opposites as a process of integration and idealization (giving life to the lifeless), whereas Eliot conceives of heterogeneity in unity as a juxtaposition of dissimilars involving wit—such as "evening sky" and "patient etherized on a table"—which Coleridge would probably call "fancy." The "significant emotion" for which Eliot searches is a concomitant of the poet's power to compel diverse materials into unity, the most effective poets combining wit and emotion.

[III]

POETRY AND BELIEF

I N HIS early criticism Eliot maintains that belief does not or should not enter into our judgment of the work; then, after a series of contradictory statements in his middle period (from about 1928 to 1935), he concludes that the belief or philosophy embodied in the work must be considered in judging the work's "greatness."[1] The early criticism involves two different, but related, solutions to the problem of belief: first, that meaning is totally embedded in the reality of the work; and second, that meaning is a vehicle of emotion (a concept similar to that of I. A. Richards).

The first solution, an identification of meaning with the reality of the work, is presented in *The Sacred Wood*. Eliot divides literature into "thought" (rhetoric) and "vision" (poetic) and argues that the two must be kept separate— either a statement of thought or a representation of events or "objects": an idea "can remain pure only by being stated simply in the form of general truth, or by being transmuted, as the attitude of Flaubert toward the small bourgeois is transformed in *Education Sentimentale*. It has there become so identified with the reality that you can no longer say what the idea is" (*SW*, p. 68). "The *Agamemnon* or *Macbeth* is . . . a statement, but of events" (*SW*, p. 65). "Mr. Conrad has no ideas, but he has a point of view, a 'world'; it can hardly be defined, but it pervades his work and is unmistakable."[2]

Eliot, however, is already moving toward the "emotional truth" concept. In his article on the Metaphysicals (1921) he implies that these poets use philosophies for emotional purposes, "to find the verbal equivalent for states of mind and feeling" (*SE*, p. 248). When he addresses himself directly to the problem of belief (1927), he complains that it "is very complicated and probably quite insoluble" (*SE*, p. 118), but he states his agreement, at least tentatively, with I. A. Richards's solution: lines are detached from their context and judged according to their emotional quality, which is independent of their truth as statements. For example, in "Shakespeare and the Stoicism of Seneca" (1927), Eliot comments on Dante and Shakespeare:

When Dante says

> *La sua voluntade e nostra pace*

it is great poetry, and there is a great philosophy behind it. When Shakespeare says

> As flies to wanton boys, are we to the gods;
> They kill us for their sport.

it is equally great poetry, though the philosophy behind it is not great. But the essential is, that each expresses in perfect language, some permanent human impulse. Emotionally, the latter is just as strong, just as true, and just as informative— just as useful and beneficial in the sense in which poetry is useful and beneficial, as the former. [*SE,* pp. 116–17]

In the same year, however, in which this passage was published, Eliot contradicts Richards's view, equating the philosophy of the poet with the meaning of the work: "Even where beliefs are not made explicit, how far can any poetry be detached from the beliefs of the poet?" "I cannot see that poetry can ever be separated from something which I should call belief, and to which I cannot see any reason for refusing the name of belief, unless we are to reshuffle names altogether."[3]

In March of the same year Eliot attempts to reconcile this viewpoint with Richards's theory: "I am not so unsophisticated as to assert that Mr. Richards's theory is *false.* It is probably quite true. Nevertheless it is only one aspect; it is a psychological theory of value, but we must also have a moral theory of value. The two are incompatible, but both must be held, and that is just the problem. If I believe, as I do believe, that the chief distinction of man is to glorify God and enjoy Him for ever, Mr. Richards's theory of value is inadequate: my advantage is that I can believe my own and his too, whereas he is limited to his own."[4]

The crux of Richards's theory is that the truth or falsity of meaning is not pertinent to the value of the poetry. If Eliot introduces a moral theory of value, regardless of how he combines it with judgment of emotion, he ceases to give assent to Richards's theory, for the truth of the meaning will indeed be pertinent to the poetry. In fact, in the preface to the 1928 edition of *The Sacred Wood,* Eliot

says, "If I ask myself . . . why I prefer the poetry of Dante
to that of Shakespeare, I should have to say, because it
seems to me to illustrate a saner attitude toward the mys-
tery of life" (p. x), although in 1933 he states that he did
not want to give the impression that he estimates "the
poetry of Shakespeare as of less value than Dante's" (*UP*,
p. 98).

In 1929 in an essay on Dante, Eliot again attempts to reconcile his theory with that of Richards. In the body of
the essay he says, "You are not called upon to believe what
Dante believed, for your belief will not give you a groat's
worth more of understanding and appreciation" (*SE*, p.
219). In a footnote to the essay Eliot repeats this idea: "I
deny, in short, that the reader must share the beliefs of
the poet in order to enjoy the poetry fully" (*SE*, p. 230).
But on the same page he states, "And I confess to considerable difficulty in analyzing my own feelings, a difficulty which makes me hesitate to accept Mr. Richards'
theory of 'pseudo-statements.'" He concludes, on the next
page: "Actually, one probably has more pleasure in the
poetry when one shares the beliefs of the poet."

As in the earlier essay, "Shakespeare and the Stoicism
of Seneca" (1927), Eliot examines lines out of context, but
this time comes to opposite conclusions: "The statement
of Keats ['Beauty is truth, truth beauty'] seems to me
meaningless: or perhaps, the fact that it is grammatically
meaningless conceals another meaning from me. The
statement of Shakespeare ['Ripeness is all'] seems to me
to have profound emotional meaning, with, at least, no
literal fallacy. And the statement of Dante ['In His will is
our peace'] seems to me *literally* true" (*SE*, p. 231). Contradicting his theory that the poet merely uses ideas to

express emotion, Eliot here judges lines of poetry as if they were scientific assertions, as if their value depends partially on whether or not they are literally true.

Eliot's dilemma even drives him into biographical judgments. In the same essay on Dante, Eliot begins with the assertion: "In my own experience of the appreciation of poetry I have always found that the less I knew about the poet and his work, before I began to read it, the better" (*SE*, p. 199). But in a footnote to the second part of the essay, in an attempt to qualify the statement that "Dante's beliefs as a man and his beliefs as a poet" should be distinguished, Eliot remarks: "If we learned, for instance, that *De Rerum Natura* was a Latin exercise which Dante had composed for relaxation after completing the *Divine Comedy*, and published under the name of one Lucretius, I am sure that our capacity for enjoying either poem would be mutilated" (*SE*, p. 230).

At times, Eliot allows his opinion of the poet's personality to influence his judgment of the poetry or simply judges the poet's personality independently of his work. For example, in *The Use of Poetry and the Use of Criticism* (1933), he says "that the biographical interest which Shelley has always excited makes it difficult to read the poetry without remembering the man: and the man was humourless, pedantic, self-centered, and sometimes almost a blackguard" (*UP*, p. 89). Milton is "antipathetic" as a man. "Either from the moralist's point of view, or from the theologian's point of view, or from the psychologist's point of view, or from that of the political philosopher, or judging by the ordinary standards of likeableness in human beings, Milton is unsatisfactory" (1936).[5] Thus, Eliot slips into a judgment of personality *apart* from the poetry—the opposite of judging "literature as literature, and not another thing."[6]

In 1930 in "Poetry and Propaganda," Eliot attempts to make his "compromise" with Richards more explicit. He says that there are two opposite views of the significance of belief in poetry, one represented by Montgomery Belgion, who maintains that a reader naturally responds to works of art as if they were propaganda, and the other by Richards, who maintains that the reader should suspend his disbelief, so that he ought "to be able to appreciate, as literature, *all* literature." But, Eliot says, "between these extremes occurs a continuous range of appreciations, each of which has its limited validity." Eliot concludes, however, that "the 'truest' philosophy is the best material for the greatest poet; so that the poet must be rated in the end both by the philosophy he realizes in poetry and by the fullness and adequacy of the realization"[7]—a reversal of Eliot's earlier view (1927) that "If Shakespeare had written according to a better philosophy he would have written worse poetry" (*SE*, p. 117).

In 1933, in *The Use of Poetry and the Use of Criticism*, Eliot abandons the standard of the "truest philosophy" and sets up a special standard for judging meaning: "When the doctrine, theory, belief, or 'view of life' presented in a poem is one which the mind of the reader can accept as coherent, mature, and founded on the facts of experience, it interposes no obstacle to the reader's enjoyment, whether it be one that he accept or deny, approve or deprecate. When it is one which the reader rejects as childish or feeble, it may, for a reader of well-developed mind, set up an almost complete check" (*UP*, p. 96).

In *After Strange Gods* (1934), however, Eliot returns to the position he had taken in "Poetry and Propaganda" (1930), contradicting the view that the acceptability of doctrines is irrelevant for the critic, and sets up a dual standard of judgment—the "literary" and the moral or theological. He remarks, "I am uncertain of my ability to criticise my contemporaries as artists; I ascended the platform of these lectures only in the role of moralist" (p. 12). In "Religion and Literature" (1935) Eliot is explicit on the duality of his standard: "Literary criticism should be completed by criticism from a definite ethical and theological standpoint. . . . The 'greatness' of literature cannot be determined solely by literary standards; though we must remember that whether it is literature or not can be determined only by literary standards" (*SE*, p. 343).

Both Cleanth Brooks and René Wellek adapt Eliot's statement in *The Use of Poetry and the Use of Criticism* to their own theories, which are in agreement with the solution proposed in Eliot's early criticism—that the literary work be viewed as an autonomous world in which meaning is fused with the reality of the work. Brooks says: "Could he [Eliot or any critic] not keep his test within the terms of the characteristic organization of the poem with some such account of affairs as this: He will regard as acceptable any poem whose unifying attitude is one which really achieves unity ('coherence'), but which unifies, not by ignoring but by taking into account the complexities and apparent contradictions of the situation concerned ('mature' and 'founded on the facts of experience')?" Wellek's formulation is similar: "though Eliot's terms go beyond aesthetic facts, one could reply that co-

herence is an aesthetic as well as logical criterion, that the
maturity of a work of art is its inclusiveness, its awareness
of complexity, and that the correspondence to reality is
registered in the work itself."[8]

This solution, which views the poem as a world *sui
generis,*[9] is apparently motivated by a desire to create
an organic theory of poetry, to prevent simple judgments
based exclusively on meaning, and to justify poetry as a
good in itself. The problem, as stated by Murray Krieger,[10]
is to show that the function of poetry is different from
that of science, yet to maintain that poetry presents a
heightened awareness of reality. The poem must "be," not
"mean"; yet it must illuminate human experience.

The criterion of illumination permits a wide latitude
in the beliefs expressed or implied by the poem. Whatever
the poet's beliefs, his poem must in some way correspond
to reality or be, in Cleanth Brooks's words, "a simulacrum
of the world of reality."[11] Although there is sharp dis-
agreement on just how the poem achieves this objective,
most contemporary critics and scholars would agree with
the early Eliot that the poem, transcending formal beliefs,
interprets some aspect of reality. The poet's interpretation
is, of course, affected by his attitudes and assumptions but
not simply determined by particular beliefs that he holds.
M. H. Abrams in the foreword of *Literature and Belief*
(1958) sums up the basic agreement of six critics on the
integral relationship between the poem and the world of
human experience: "The common ground, express or implied, is that a work of literature is to be apprehended
for its inherent and terminal values; but that, in so far as
it represents human beings and human experiences, it

involves assumptions and beliefs and sympathies with which a large measure of concurrence is indispensable for the reading of literature as literature and not another thing" (p. x). As Abrams makes clear, this concurrence relates to attitudes toward human nature, not to philosophical agreement. Regardless of how much these critics may disagree in their philosophical orientation, they approach poetry with a common set of human values. They would agree with Eliot's statement that the poet should have a "firm grasp of human experience" (*SE*, p. 256) but reject his later proposal that the philosophy implied by the poem be judged separately from the poem.

[IV]

THE CRITICAL PRACTICE

Eliot's Critical Ideal

CRITICISM, Eliot says (1923), "must always profess an end in view, which, roughly speaking, appears to be the elucidation of works of art and the correction of taste" (*SE*, p. 13). Criticism involves a "minute and scrupulous examination of felicity and blemish, line by line" (*UP*, p. 25) and an explanation of the work, including "its conditions, its setting, its genesis" (*SE*, p. 20). Although Eliot does not rule out the method of exegesis, he does not suggest it. His emphasis is on the evaluation of style and the provision of facts, with the qualification that the concentration on facts should not become an interest in biography for its own sake: "The chief task [of explanation] is the presentation of relevant historical facts which the reader is not assumed to know" (*SE*, p. 122).

Criticism is an attempt to carry out "an honest inquiry as far as the data permit" (*SE*, pp. 21–22). The critic should not state his judgments but "simply elucidate: the reader will form the correct judgment for himself" (*SW*, p. 11). "English criticism is inclined to argue or persuade rather than to state; and, instead of forcing the subject to expose himself, these critics have left in their work an undissolved residuum of their own good taste, which, however impeccable, is something that requires our faith" (*SE*, p. 181).

Eliot believes that the critic should take part with his fellow critics in the "common pursuit of true judgment" (*SE*, p. 14), but he advises him to bestow "a method, rather than a judgment" (*SE*, p. 181):

The work of the critic is almost wholly comprehended in the "complementary activities" of comparison and analysis. The one activity implies the other; and together they provide the only way of asserting standards and of isolating a writer's peculiar merits. In the dogmatic, or lazy, mind comparison is supplied by judgment, analysis replaced by appreciation. Judgment and appreciation are merely tolerable avocations, no part of the critic's serious business. If the critic has performed his laboratory work well, his understanding will be evidence of appreciation; but his work is by the intelligence not the emotions. The judgment will also take place in the reader's mind, not in the critic's explicit statement. When he judges or appreciates he simply (perhaps from a legitimate compulsion to spare time or thought) is missing out a link in the exposition.[1]

The main danger in criticism, according to Eliot, is interpretation: "in this type of writing there are thousands of impostures. Instead of insight, you get a fiction. Your test is to apply it [the critic's interpretation] again and again to the original, with your view of the original to guide you. But there is no one to guarantee your com-

petence, and once again we find ourselves in a dilemma"
(*SE*, p. 20).

Although Eliot, in an essay on Wilson Knight (1930),
qualifies his view of interpretation, saying that in some
instances it cannot be avoided, he still regards interpretation as undesirable:

> So, finally, the sceptical practitioner of verse tends to limit
> his criticism of poetry to the appreciation of vocabulary and
> syntax, the analysis of line, metric and cadence; to stick as
> closely to the more trustworthy senses as possible.
> Or rather, tends to *try* to do this. For this exact and humble
> appreciation is only one ideal never quite arrived at or even so
> far as approximated consistently maintained. The restless
> demon in us drives us also to "interpret" whether we will or
> not.[2]

Eliot's "comparison and analysis" is an analysis of the
work as art, particularly of language. His emphasis on
analysis is based on two assumptions: that interpretation
cannot be substantiated and that the primary function of
the critic is to examine the work as art. The assumption
that interpretation cannot be substantiated fails, however,
to take into account the fact that neither interpretation nor
analysis is absolutely verifiable; both activities require
criteria based on the principle of probability. When a
critic makes analytical evaluations, he does so according
to a standard; the facts he uses are important only as they
are related to judgment. The critic also interprets according to a standard, and he uses facts related to judgment. Eliot says that the practitioner of verse *qua* critic
tries "to stick as closely to the more trustworthy senses as
possible," "to the appreciation of vocabulary and syntax,
the analysis of line, metric and cadence." Eliot may feel

more competent in this area, but objectively he has no more means of verification than the interpreter. Although the implications of a work's meaning are difficult to establish, they are no more so than judgment of a line's intensity or complexity or illumination.

Eliot's second assumption, that the primary function of the critic is to examine the work as art, is related to a basic principle of much contemporary criticism—the belief that since a work should be judged only as art, it should be viewed only as art. But any kind of work can be interpreted, without examination of its esthetic qualities. Further, if we judge on the basis of the number of books and articles published, interpretation occupies a much larger place in the critical function than evaluation. Although evaluation is important, the most pressing problem in the study of literature is interpretation, the principles and methods by which we come to an understanding of literary works.

Eliot suggests the substitution of "relevant historical facts" for interpretation (*SE*, p. 122). He distinguishes between the work of art *qua* work of art and interpretation of the work: "*Qua* work of art, the work of art cannot be interpreted; there is nothing to interpret; we can only criticise it according to standards, in comparison to other works of art" (*SE*, p. 122). The critic merely provides the relevant facts, apparently leaving the reader to make the interpretation for himself. If the critic, however, decides what is relevant, he is making an interpretation. Eliot, in fact, after objecting to interpretation (in the essay on *Hamlet*), proceeds to make an interpretation, using the fact that Shakespeare based *Hamlet* on an earlier play to conclude that Shakespeare attempts to impose the motive "of a mother's guilt upon her son" on the simple revenge motive of the earlier play. It is true that Eliot moves from interpretation to evaluation, judging Shakespeare's attempt as unsuccessful, but he first makes an interpretation.

Interpretations can be made, and are often made, without reference to evaluation; but evaluations, at least of works in their totality, require reference to interpretation. Eliot's view of evaluation (in his early criticism) is too limited, bound by his concern with line, meter, and cadence. Interpretation, which Eliot wishes to eliminate, is not only extremely valuable in itself but is necessary to evaluation. One could even argue that we are more likely to achieve objectivity in the area of interpretation than in the area of evaluation. Eliot's opposition to interpretation is based on the idea that analysis is closer to facts than the interpretation of meaning. Both, however, depend on facts, and both are related to judgment, which cannot be eliminated.

Eliot's Generalizations

In his own critical practice Eliot makes frequent interpretations, usually in one or two sentences: for example, that *The Jew of Malta* is a savage farce (*SE,* p. 105), that the tragedy of *The Changeling* is Beatrice's habituation to her sin (*SE,* p. 143), that the central meaning of *Hamlet* is found in the effect of a mother's guilt upon her son (*SE,* p. 124), or that Dante's hell is not a place but a state of mind (*SE,* p. 211). The detailed elucidation of meaning is absent from Eliot's criticism, although detailed evaluation of style, particularly in his early criticism, is paramount. His elucidation is usually confined to an examination of imagery, language, and rhythm, accompanied by evaluation, as in his criticism of Marlowe's plays—"the facile use of resonant names," "a new and important conversational tone in the dialogue of Faustus with the Devil," or "style which secures its emphasis by always hesitating on the edge of caricature at the right moment" (SE, pp. 103–105).

In his criticism of authors Eliot makes numerous judgments, frequently without any attempt to substantiate them: "Thomas Hobbes was one of those extraordinary little upstarts whom the chaotic motions of the Renaissance tossed into an eminence which they hardly deserved and have never lost" (SE, p. 312). "When I add to the name of Daudet, that of a master of a very different and much more austere style, Charles Maurras, I have named with Whibley the three best writers of invective of their time" (SE, p. 445). "In the whole range of literature covered, Swinburne makes hardly more than two judgments which can be reversed or even questioned" (SW, p. 19). A "large part" of Whitman's content is "claptrap."[3] "The essays of Emerson are already an encumbrance."[4]

The question is not the validity or invalidity of these judgments, but Eliot's method of presenting them without any attempt at substantiation. The same type of generalization occurs throughout the Selected Essays—beginning, for example, with Eliot's contrast of Classicism and Romanticism, "the difference seems to me rather the difference between the complete and the fragmentary, the adult and the immature, the orderly and the chaotic" (SE, p. 15), and ending with his evaluation of the main task of education, "The first educational task of the communities should be the preservation of education within the cloister, uncontaminated by the deluge of barbarism outside" (SE,

p. 460). Although a critic cannot completely avoid unsupported generalizations, particularly in references to
several writers (designed to clarify the work under discussion), he should at least hold these generalizations to
a minimum.

Eliot, particularly in his early criticism, is quite conscious of the problem—"The dogmatic critic, who lays
down a rule, who affirms a value, has left his labour in-
complete" (*SW*, p. 11)—but in his practice Eliot is frequently oblivious of the necessity of evidence or even
argument. His dogmatism is most apparent in Section VI
(on religion) in *Selected Essays*, and it increases in his
later religious and sociological works: *After Strange Gods*
(1934), *The Idea of a Christian Society* (1939), and *Notes
towards the Definition of Culture* (1948). In *After Strange
Gods* he proclaims that "In a society like ours, wormeaten
with Liberalism, the only thing possible for a person with
strong convictions is to state a point of view and leave it
at that."[5]

The extreme of the dogmatic approach, as M. C. Bradbrook has noted,[6] occurs in Eliot's references to Thomas
Rymer. The first two references appear in footnotes, one
in the essay on *Hamlet*, the other in "Four Elizabethan
Dramatists": "I have never, by the way, seen a cogent
refutation of Thomas Rymer's objections to *Othello*" (*SE*,
p. 121). "This [an objection to the three sisters and Ban-
quo's ghost appearing in the same play] will appear to
be an objection as pedantic as that of Thomas Rymer to
Othello. But Rymer makes out a very good case" (*SE*, p.
97). Elsewhere Eliot remarks that "We cannot quite say
the first serious criticism [Dryden's], because there is for
instance the contemporary criticism of Thomas Rymer—

a critic of whom Dryden speaks highly, and of whom I should be tempted to speak more highly still."[7]

"The real corrupters," Eliot tells us, "are those who supply opinion or fancy" (*SE*, p. 21). Perhaps Eliot's realization of the discrepancy between his theory of criticism and the bulk of his practice has led him to say on at least four different occasions that the criticism of a poet should be evaluated in relation to his poetry: "When the critics are themselves poets, it may be suspected that they have formed their critical statements with a view to justifying their poetic practice" (*UP*, p. 29); "their pronouncements should usually be considered in relation to their own poems"; "we must return to the scholar for ascertainment of facts, and to the more detached critic for impartial judgment."[8]

Eliot's Prose Style

Complementary to his critical ideal of "a sense of fact," Eliot sets clarity and force as his ideal of prose style—an ability to keep one's "eye on the object." "For interest in what one has to say, rather than conforming to or revolting from a conventional manner, is the essential thing: an interest in the subject, and a grasp of it, which give a proper intellectual and emotional balance, and prevent both conventionality and eccentricity."[9]

Eliot criticizes the poetic style of Sir Thomas Browne and praises the style of Lancelot Andrewes, because of its "ordonnance, or arrangement and structure, precision in the use of words, and relevant intensity" (*SE*, p. 302). Eliot himself writes an unadorned prose, distinguished by an occasional use of effective metaphor, such as "the blossoms of Beaumont and Fletcher's imagination draw no sustenance from the soil, but are cut and slightly withered flowers stuck into sand" (*SE*, p. 135), or "the ghost of some simple metre should lurk behind the arras in even the 'freest' verse,"[10] or "the suggestiveness is the aura around a bright clear centre" (*SE*, p. 259).

But Eliot often fails in his prose to achieve his ideal of clarity. In spite of his reputation as a precisionist in style, his style has the weakness which Stanley Hyman describes as "a fuzzy and contradictory thinking that results in key terms that are meaningless or nebulous (or a nebulous terminology that results in fuzzy and contradictory writing, depending on how you look at it)."[11] For example, such terms as "objective correlative," "dissociation of sensibility," and "impersonal"—all basic to Eliot's theory of poetry—are not clearly and sharply defined. Eliot's style is best when he writes about lines of poetry. When he discusses poetic theory, he seems to be attempting to think through the problem as he writes. He complains that he can never reread his own prose "without acute embarrassment": "I shirk the task, and consequently may not take account of all the assertions to which I have at one time or another committed myself; I may often repeat what I have said before, and I may often contradict myself."[12]

The Essay on Marlowe: An Analysis of Line and Cadence

We can observe Eliot's method of stylistic evaluation, his analysis of line and cadence (typical of his early critical practice), by examining his essay on Marlowe (1919). The essay begins with a number of generalizations—that Swinburne is partially correct (he should not have ignored Kyd and Surrey) in saying that Marlowe was the father of English tragedy, the creator of English blank verse, and the teacher of Shakespeare; that blank verse reached its height in Shakespeare's lifetime and has retrogressed since Milton's "erection of the Chinese Wall"; that Marlowe has a personal tone and that his blank verse, therefore, differs to some extent from that of the dramatists who come after him; and that the vices of style of Shakespeare and Marlowe may be described as Shakespeare's "tortured perverse ingenuity of images which dissipates . . . the imagination" and Marlowe's "simple huffe-snuffe bombast," although Marlowe was turning the vice into a virtue.

After comparing a passage from *The Faerie Queene* (I.vii. 32) and *Tamburlaine* (Part II, IV. iv), Eliot concludes that the comparison shows that Marlowe's talent, like that of most poets, "was partly synthetic" and that some particularly lyric effects were achieved in *Tamburlaine:* "the combination produced results which could not be repeated. I do not think that it can be claimed that Peele had any influence here" (*SE*, p. 102). His conclusion to the Spenser-Marlowe relationship in *Tamburlaine* is that "Marlowe gets into blank verse the melody of Spenser, and he gets a new driving power by reinforcing the sentence period against the line period" (*SE*, p. 104).

"In *Faustus* Marlowe went farther: he broke up the line, to a gain in intensity, in the last soliloquy; and he developed a new and important conversational tone in the dialogues of Faustus with the devil." Then Eliot says that he will limit his discussion to two plays—"One of which has been misunderstood and the other underrated"—*The*

Jew of Malta and *Dido, Queen of Carthage. The Jew of Malta* exemplifies a tone suitable to "savage comic humour" and *Dido* a "style which secures its emphasis by always hesitating on the edge of caricature at the right moment" (*SE*, pp. 104–105).

The essay concludes with the judgment that Marlowe was moving in a direction "quite un-Shakespearean . . . toward this intense and serious and indubitably great poetry, which . . . attains its effects by something not unlike caricature" (*SE*, p. 106). The implication is that Marlowe's style in each play is different and that Eliot is describing its "development," from the lyricism of *Tamburlaine* to the intensity and conversational tone of *Faustus* to the "savage comic humour" of *The Jew of Malta* to the "caricature" of *Dido*. But *Dido* is commonly thought to be the first play that Marlowe wrote.[13] Yet Eliot says that in *Dido* "there is progress," that there is a development from a tone to suit the farce of *The Jew of Malta* to *Dido's* "newer style . . . which secures its emphasis by hesitating on the edge of caricature."

The thesis of the Marlowe essay is "that Marlowe exercised a strong influence over later drama, . . . and that when Shakespeare borrowed from him, which was pretty often at the beginning, Shakespeare either made something inferior or something different" (*SE*, p. 100). But we learn nothing of Marlowe's influence on later drama; and though Eliot tells us of Marlowe's "new driving power" in *Tamburlaine* and *Faustus,* evidently a part of the development of blank verse, he suddenly drops this line of thought and points out Marlowe's aberration, a personal type of "caricature," which is "quite un-Shakespearean." Although he contrasts Shakespeare's style, in one passage, with Marlowe's, he makes no mention of Shakespeare's borrowings, the making of "something inferior or something different."

Eliot's essay, in its failure to substantiate its generalizations, demonstrates that technical analysis in itself does not meet his objections to interpretation. Analytical criticism, even at its best, is only one type of criticism, its value depending on its relevance to a significant illumination of the work. When analysis is unsubstantiated, it is no more dependable than vague interpretations or appreciations.

The Essay on Marvell:
An Analysis of Imagery

One of the best essays of Eliot is that on Andrew Marvell (1921), which epitomizes Eliot's early method of studying a poet's style through the comparison and analysis of imagery. He intends the essay to demonstrate a general thesis: that the purpose of criticism is not "to determine rank" but to isolate the essential qualities of a poet's works (SE, p. 251). Although this type of criticism does not constitute as large a part of Eliot's criticism as is generally thought, it is what he does best: citing lines of poetry and comparing them with other lines and then drawing conclusions about their stylistic qualities. Although he does not eliminate unsupported generalizations, he subordinates them to a detailed examination of imagery and language.

The essential quality that he finds in Marvell is metaphysical wit, "a tough reasonableness beneath the slight lyric grace" (SE, p. 252). Whereas Milton possesses magniloquence, and Dryden wit, Marvell possesses both qualities. Before examining this special quality of Marvell, Eliot attempts to explain how Marvell differs from Milton in that he was a moderate Puritan, not of the "flock of Zeal-of-the-land Busy," and therefore he "speaks more clearly and unequivocally with the voice of his literary age than does Milton" (*SE*, p. 253).

After he has established to his own satisfaction that not all Puritans, even though "Liberal Practitioners," were a part of the "Dissidence of Dissent," Eliot turns to an examination of "To His Coy Mistress," which he says has the commonplace theme of Herrick's "To the Virgins" and possesses "the savage austerity of Lucretius and the intense levity of Catullus" (*SE*, p. 253). The "wit of Marvell renews the theme . . . in the variety and order of the images"—such as "world enough and time," "ten years before the Flood," and "Till the conversion of the Jews." The poem magnifies the original fancy through a "succession of concentrated images" and "turns suddenly with that surprise which has been one of the most important means of poetic effect since Homer," as in the lines,

> But at my back I always hear
> Time's wingèd chariot hurrying near,
> And yonder all before us lie
> Deserts of vast eternity.

In the next paragraph Eliot returns to his thesis of metaphysical wit. He cites other lines from the poem and attempts to define the quality of Marvell's wit, which he concludes is an "alliance of levity and seriousness (by which the seriousness is intensified)"—a quality found in Gautier, Baudelaire, Laforgue, Catullus, Jonson, Propertius, and Ovid: "It is a quality of a sophisticated literature; a quality which expands in English literature just at the moment before the English mind altered; it is not a quality which we should expect Puritanism to encourage" (SE, pp. 254–56). This statement alludes to Eliot's idea of the dissociation of sensibility, although he does not use the term in this essay. By the time we get to Gray and Collins, "the sophistication remains only in the language, and has disappeared from the feeling," a sophistication characterized by a "firm grasp of human experience" and completed by "the religious comprehension" (SE, p. 256)—an attitude that is cynical but untired, combining seriousness and levity or wit and emotion.

Eliot next presents his distinction between imagination and fancy: the imagination creates integrated images, whereas fancy creates images that support only themselves and are therefore blemishes, such as "the leaden house does sweat" or "Antipodes in shoes" (canoes on the heads of salmon-fishers). Eliot's concept of fancy is narrower than Coleridge's; for he would classify as witty and imaginative many images falling under Coleridge's category of fancy (defined by Coleridge as associated images). The images of "To His Coy Mistress" not only are witty but also satisfy "the elucidation of Imagination given by Coleridge: . . . 'the balance or reconcilement of opposite or discordant qualities'" (SE, p. 256).

The other quality of Marvell that Eliot admires is his precision of images, in contrast to William Morris' vagueness. Eliot compares Marvell's "The Nymph and the Fawn" to Morris' "The Nymph's Song to Hylas," concluding that Marvell's emotion, like his objects of emotion, is precise, whereas Morris' is vague. Marvell's poem, al-

though "appearing more slight, is the more serious" (*SE,*
p. 258). Also, Marvell's poetry is more suggestive, for
suggestiveness is dependent on precision: "we are inclined
to infer that the suggestiveness is the aura around a bright
clear centre, that you cannot have the aura alone" (*SE,*
p. 259)—an idea frequently advanced by T. E. Hulme in
his battle against Romantic "vagueness and mistiness."

Eliot, like Hulme, ascribes this vagueness, which was
accompanied by a loss in wit, to the attempt of the Romantic poets to "construct a dream-world," an attempt
"which alters English poetry so greatly in the nineteenth
century" (*SE,* p. 259)—another allusion to his concept of
the dissociation of sensibility: after the seventeenth century, poetry lost metaphysical wit and became unbalanced, either pure wit or pure seriousness. Dryden and
Milton are cited as examples: "Dryden was great in wit, as
Milton in magniloquence; but the former, by isolating this
quality and making it by itself into great poetry, and the
latter, by coming to dispense with it altogether, may
perhaps have injured the language" (*SE,* p. 260). Eliot
does not evaluate Marvell as a better poet than Milton
or Dryden, but he believes that the loss of metaphysical
wit was damaging to the poetic tradition.

The rest of the Marvell essay is devoted to an attempt
to define Marvell's quality of wit: "an equipoise, a balance
and proportion of tones" or "shades of feeling to contrast
and unite." Eliot cites Cowley's definition of it as unity
in diversity: "all things must be/Yet all things there agree"
(*SE,* p. 261). Wit is not erudition or cynicism, "though it
has .a kind of toughness which may be confused with
cynicism by the tender-minded. . . . It involves, probably,
a recognition, implicit in the expression of every experi-

ence, of other kinds of experience which are possible, which we find as clearly in the greatest as in poets like Marvell." This constant inspection and criticism of experience leads to a balance between seriousness and levity. Marvell never takes "a subject too seriously or too lightly" (*SE*, p. 262). His "intellectual" poetry involves a combination of wit (in the sense of levity) and intensity. Today, "we find serious poets who are afraid of acquiring wit, lest they lose intensity. . . . By whatever name we call it, and however we define that name, it is something precious and needed and apparently extinct" (*SE*, p. 263).

The Marvell essay contains ideas which have been influential in contemporary criticism—on the precision of imagery, the integration of image and idea, the combination of wit and emotion, and the poetry of "inclusion," which expresses counterbalancing attitudes. It represents Eliot at his best—a poet writing literary essays which compare and analyze lines of poetry, attempting to define the essential characteristics of the poet under discussion. Eliot's insights are mostly in the details of his analysis, as in his characterization of Marvell as a poet who contrasts and unites shades of feeling or of Donne as a poet who possesses a "direct sensuous apprehension of thought" (*SE*, p. 246). The concept of "the dissociation of sensibility," which grows out of the discussion (defined in "The Metaphysical Poets"), reflects both Eliot's philosophical position and his special interests as a poet: his belief that thought (idea) and feeling (image) should be integral (a concept presumably borrowed from the philosopher F. H. Bradley) and his preference for a poetry that is both witty and emotional.

[V]

THE SOCIAL CRITICISM

Literature and Morality

IT WOULD have been difficult in 1920, when *The Sacred Wood* appeared, to predict that Eliot, the advocate of the criticism of poetry as poetry and not another thing, would concentrate most of his attention after 1930 on political, social, and religious criticism, particularly in *After Strange Gods* (1934), *The Idea of a Christian Society* (1939), and *Notes towards the Definition of Culture* (1948). But as early as 1921 Eliot asserts that the poet's vision should be completed by religious comprehension. His preoccupation during the twenties with the problem of poetry and belief involves a conflict between his desire to view poetry as poetry and his preference for the poetry that expresses ideas with which he agrees—for example, the poetry of Dante as distinguished from that of Shakespeare. In an attempt to resolve his dilemma, Eliot sets up a dual standard of judgment, the literary and the moral.

In *After Strange Gods* Eliot disclaims any concern with literary criticism, saying that he speaks "only in the role of moralist. . . . I do not wish to preach only to the converted, but primarily to those who, never having applied moral principles to literature quite explicitly—perhaps even having conscientiously believed that they ought not to apply them in this way to 'works of art'—are possibly convertible."[1] He says that the writers he discusses are "among the best" and that the extent to which he criticizes them shows his respect for them.

Eliot begins his discussion of moral problems in literature by analyzing three short stories: "Bliss," by Katherine Mansfield; "The Shadow in the Rose Garden," by D. H. Lawrence; and "The Dead," by James Joyce. Mansfield concentrates on feeling, without "suggestion of any moral issue of good and evil, and within the setting this is quite right." She "has handled perfectly the *minimum* material" (*ASG*, p. 36). The story by D. H. Lawrence typifies the relations of Lawrence's men and women, who have no "moral or social sense." Lawrence's characters, "who are supposed to be recognisably human beings, betray no respect for, or even awareness of, moral obligations, and seem to be unfurnished with even the most commonplace kind of conscience" (p. 37). In Joyce's "The Dead" a husband learns something about the nature of love when his wife tells him about a boy who loved her when she was a girl. From this evidence Eliot concludes that Lawrence is heretical and that Joyce manifests an orthodox sensibility: "We are not concerned with the authors' *beliefs*, but with orthodoxy of sensibility and with the sense of tradition. . . . And Lawrence is for my purposes, an almost perfect exam-

ple of the heretic. And the most ethically orthodox of the
more eminent writers of my time is Mr. Joyce" (p. 38).

The writers with unorthodox sensibilities can best be
understood by examining "the type of Protestantism which
surrounded their infancy, and the precise state of decay
which it had reached" (*ASG,* p. 38). Irving Babbitt, for example, tried "to compensate for the lack of living tradition
by a herculean, but purely intellectual and individual ef-
fort" (p. 40). Another "individualist, and still more a liber-
tarian," is Ezra Pound, who is, according to Eliot, "probably
the most important living poet in our language" (p. 42). In
his *Draft of XXX Cantos,* Eliot continues, Pound creates un-
real people in a "perfectly comfortable" hell because he
fails to distinguish "between individual responsibility and
circumstances in Hell, between essential Evil and social
accidents" (p. 43):

At this point I shall venture to generalise, and suggest that with
the disappearance of the idea of Original Sin, with the disappearance of the idea of intense moral struggle, the human
beings presented to us both in poetry and in prose fiction today, and more patently among the serious writers than in the
underworld of letters, tend to become less and less real. It is
in fact in moments of moral and spiritual struggle depending
upon spiritual sanctions, rather than in those "bewildering
minutes" in which we are all very much alike, that men and
women come nearest to being real. If you do away with this
struggle, and maintain that by tolerance, benevolence, in-
offensiveness and a redistribution or increase of purchasing
power, combined with a devotion, on the part of an élite, to
Art, the world will be as good as anyone could require, then
you must expect human beings to become more and more
vaporous. [*ASG,* p. 42]

Another writer of unorthodox sensibility is Yeats, particularly the younger Yeats. In attempting to create his own tradition, a private mythology, Yeats cut himself off from common experience and became eccentric: His "'supernatural world' was the wrong supernatural world. It was not a world of spiritual significance, not a world of real Good and Evil, of holiness or sin, but a highly sophisticated lower mythology summoned, like a physician, to supply the fading pulse of poetry with some transient stimulant so that the dying patient may utter his last words" (*ASG*, p. 46). The later Yeats outgrew this private mythology, although he failed to arrive at a "central and universal philosophy" (p. 47).

Even a religious poet like Gerard Hopkins lacks the advantage of those poets who inherited a central tradition: "Hopkins is not a religious poet in the more important sense in which I have elsewhere maintained Baudelaire to be a religious poet; or in the sense in which I find Villon to be a religious poet; or in the sense in which I consider Mr. Joyce's work to be penetrated with Christian feeling." The main struggle of our time is "to concentrate, not to dissipate; to renew our association with traditional wisdom; to re-establish a vital connexion between the individual and the race; the struggle, in a word, against Liberalism: from all this Hopkins is a little apart, and in this Hopkins has very little aid to offer us" (*ASG*, p. 48).

The imposition of a personal view of life is "part of the whole movement of several centuries towards the aggrandisement and exploitation of *personality*" (*ASG*, p. 53). George Eliot, for example, possesses "moral insight and passion," but her individualistic morals are to be deplored:

"when morals cease to be a matter of tradition and orthodoxy—that is, of the habits of the community, formulated,
corrected, and elevated by the continuous thought and direction of the Church—and when each man is to elaborate
his own, then *personality* becomes a thing of alarming importance" (p. 54). Thomas Hardy "represents an interesting
example of a powerful personality uncurbed by an institutional attachment or by submission to any objective beliefs." Hardy wrote merely for the sake of self-expression,
"and the self which he had to express" is not "a particularly wholesome or edifying matter of communication."
Hardy's "characters come alive" only "in their emotional
paroxyms," exemplifying the romantic belief "that there is
something admirable in violent emotion for its own sake,
whatever the emotion or whatever its object" (pp. 54–55).
For example, in "Barbara of the House of Grebe" Hardy
introduces us "into a world of pure Evil. The tale would
seem to have been written solely to provide a satisfaction
for some morbid emotion" (p. 58).

    "I doubt," Eliot states, "whether what I am saying can
convey very much to anyone for whom the doctrine of
Original Sin is not a very real and tremendous thing" (*ASG*,
p. 57). Like T. E. Hulme, Eliot contrasts institutional orthodoxy to "the Inner Light, the most untrustworthy and
deceitful guide that ever offered itself to wandering humanity" (p. 59). The vision of D. H. Lawrence, a follower
of the "Inner Light," is "spiritually sick" (p. 60). "Lawrence's work may appeal . . . to the sick and debile and
confused; and will appeal not to what remains of health in
them, but to their sickness" (p. 61). The only acceptable
alternative to individualism is orthodoxy: "Tradition by itself is not enough; it must be perpetually criticised and

brought up to date under the supervision of what I call orthodoxy" (p. 62).

Eliot bases his argument in *After Strange Gods* on the desirability of having an "orthodox sensibility," saying that the writer's work suffers when it lacks this sensibility, that it fails to achieve the reality and depth that orthodoxy would give it. He judges Lawrence's characters, for example, as shallow because they are not involved in essential moral struggles, and he criticizes the works of both Lawrence and Hardy for their individualistic morality, their exaltation of personality for its own sake.

In the second chapter of *After Strange Gods* (dealing primarily with Joyce, Babbitt, Pound, Yeats, and Hopkins), Eliot maintains that the lack of an orthodox moral perspective weakens the literary work, even though he admires many of the qualities of these writers' works. Although he applies a dual standard of value, he emphasizes literary qualities in his judgment of the work, asserting that Ezra Pound, in spite of a faulty moral vision, is the greatest living poet writing in English. In the third chapter, in which Eliot examines the influence of the "diabolical" on literature, he emphasizes morality, deploring the unhealthy influences of the works of Lawrence and Hardy.

Eliot applies moral standards to the judgment of literature in two ways: as moral quality affects the value of the work and as it influences the beliefs and behavior of the reader. He says that the faulty moral vision of certain writers (for example, Pound, Yeats, and Lawrence) weakens works that possess literary merit: Pound does not deal with "essential Evil," so his poetry lacks the depth that moral vision would have given it; Yeats's mythology, substituted for religious vision, induces artificiality; and Lawrence's preoccupation with emotion for its own sake creates amoral characters who are hardly recognizable as human beings. As for the influence of the work of literature on the reader, Eliot says that many writers, including himself, have probably had a negative moral effect. His major examples of negative influence are representations, especially in the works of Lawrence and Hardy, of emotion for its own sake, particularly of emotions related to cruelty.

Eliot's concern with the effect of moral quality on the work of art is an esthetic concern, for he maintains that its esthetic value is weakened, that the work loses depth because of its shallow moral vision. But his concern with the effect of the work on the reader is not an esthetic concern. Even the most pragmatic critic (interested essentially in how the work affects the reader) must return to the work itself and analyze the qualities that produce the effect. Eliot's interest in the problem of effect stems from his interests as a religious spokesman who wishes to influence people to believe and behave in certain ways. His purpose in *After Strange Gods* is to combat prophets of individualism, heretics who "follow their own spirit" (*ASG*, p. 61). The enemy—exaltation of personality in literature—is an old one for Eliot. But his earlier objections to personality were literary, concerned with the negative ways in which the direct expression of personality affects the literary work. In *After Strange Gods* he is concerned with the moral harm caused by the expression of personality, arguing that the remedy to the situation is a religious orthodoxy to guide the writer's moral perspective:

The personality thus expressed, the personality which fascinates us in the work of philosophy or art, tends naturally to be the *unregenerate* personality, partly self-deceived and partly irresponsible, and because of its freedom, terribly *limited* by prejudice and self-conceit, capable of much good or great mischief according to the natural goodness or impurity of the man: and we are all, naturally, impure. All that I have been able to do here is to suggest that there are standards of criticism, not ordinarily in use, which we may apply to whatever is offered to us as works of philosophy or of art, which might help to render them safer and more profitable for us. [*ASG*, p. 63]

Eliot's Ideal Society

Eliot found in religion the hope to sustain him in a life that he felt to be chaotic and painful, feelings often expressed in his poetry. His attitude is revealed, for example, in his praise (in 1929) of the *Vita Nuova* for its sense of reality: "not to expect more from *life* than it can give or more from *human* beings than they can give; to look to *death* for what life cannot give" (*SE*, p. 235). But just as he objects to the display of personality in literature, he objects to personal religion, to what he often refers to as the "Inner Light." He puts his faith in organized religion, in religious orthodoxy as it has been institutionally established. What is important to him, he says, are the dogmas of religion, particularly the dogma of original sin. The two fundamental principles of his religion are that man is essentially evil, disciplined only by institutions, and that this world, whatever its particular economic and political arrangements, is unimportant in relation to eternity.

In *The Idea of a Christian Society* (1939), Eliot describes the type of society he would like to see established. What is most important to him is that the society be religious. In

attempting to persuade others of the desirability of his
ideal, he asserts that a Christian society is the only alternative to a socialist or fascist society. He sees both Germany
and the Soviet Union as characterized primarily by pagan-
ism, by concentration on material welfare. He does not
analyze the economic and political realities of these societies, but designates them as threats from which a Christian
society can save both England and the United States.

Eliot begins his discussion of his proposed Christian society by commending Christian sociologists: "those writers
who criticize our economic system in the light of Christian
ethics." They are reformers who demonstrate "the incom-
patibility of Christian principle and a great deal of our
social practice," appealing to the "spirit of justice and humanity with which most of us profess to be inspired."[2] The
changes advocated by these writers "can recommend
themselves to any intelligent and disinterested person, and
do not require a Christian society to carry them into effect,
or Christian belief to render them acceptable." But Eliot is
concerned "only secondarily with the changes in economic
organisation." His primary interest "is a change in our
social attitude, such a change only as could bring about
anything worthy to be called a Christian Society," although the creation of a Christian Society would compel
changes (not specified by Eliot) "in our organisation of
industry and commerce and financial credit" (*ICS*, p. 7).

Eliot presents only two possible alternatives to the present situation in England or America: a Christian society or
a pagan society like that of Germany or Russia:

It is my contention that we have today a culture which is
mainly negative, but which, so far as it is positive, is still Chris-

tian. I do not think that it can remain negative, because a negative culture has ceased to be efficient in a world where economic as well as spiritual forces are proving the efficiency of
cultures which, even when pagan, are positive; and I believe
that the choice before us is between the formation of a new
Christian culture, and the acceptance of a pagan one. Both
involve radical changes; but I believe that the majority of us,
if we could be faced immediately with all the changes which
will only be accomplished in several generations, would prefer
Christianity. [ICS, p. 10]

Eliot addresses himself to those readers who are aware
that "great changes must come, but are not sure either of
what is inevitable, or of what is probable, or of what is de-
sirable." It is vain to speak to those "who cannot believe
that things will ever be very different from what they are
at the moment" (ICS, p. 11).

The present society of the Western World, in Eliot's
view, stands for "Liberalism" and "Democracy." Although
some people have argued "that democracy is the only
regime compatible with Christianity; . . . the word is not
abandoned by sympathisers with the government of Germany." Defenders of the German system "can make out a
plausible case for maintaining that what we have is not
democracy, but financial oligarchy." It is likely that states
such as England and America will develop into "a kind
of totalitarian democracy"—a democracy in form only
(ICS, p. 12). What these states are permeated with, Eliot
ₛ. ys, is Liberalism, a movement defined more by what it is
against than by what it is for:

By destroying traditional social habits of the people, by dis-
solving their natural collective consciousness into individual

constituents, by licensing the opinions of the most foolish, by substituting instruction for education, by encouraging cleverness rather than wisdom, the upstart rather than the qualified, by fostering a notion of *getting on* to which the alternative is a hopeless apathy, Liberalism can prepare the way for that which is its own negation: the artificial, mechanised or brutalised control which is a desperate remedy for its chaos. [*ICS*, p. 13]

Liberalism is a negative force known by its rejections, "and with nothing to destroy," it "is left with nothing to uphold and with nowhere to go" (*ICS*, p. 13). Liberalism, in fact, has no political philosophy, for "a party with a political philosophy is a revolutionary party" (p.15). The choice is "between a pagan, and necessarily stunted culture, and a religious, and necessarily imperfect culture."

The attitudes and beliefs of Liberalism "are destined to disappear, are already disappearing." Liberalism belongs "to an age of free exploitation which has passed; . . . Out of Liberalism itself come philosophies which deny it." For example, the preserves of "private life" that are so important to Liberal thought may imperceptibly become "smaller and smaller, and may eventually disappear altogether" (*ICS*, p. 16). What will be left is the term "democracy," which still "has a Liberal connotation of 'freedom.' But totalitarianism can retain the terms 'freedom' and 'democracy' and give them its own meaning; and its right to them is not so easily disproved as minds inflamed by passion suppose. We are in danger of finding ourselves with nothing to stand for except a *dislike* of everything maintained by Germany and/or Russia" (p. 17).

Our political philosophy, according to Eliot, has lost its cogency and conviction. We do not realize, for example, that the "fundamental objection to fascist doctrine, the one which we conceal from ourselves because it might condemn ourselves as well, is that it is pagan. . . . There are still other objections, to oppression and violence and cruelty, but however strongly we feel, these are objections to means and not to ends." We try "to disguise the fact that our aims, like Germany's, are materialistic."

The "only alternative to a progressive and insidious adaptation to totalitarian worldliness for which the pace is already set, is to aim at a Christian society" (*ICS*, 18). The Liberal idea that religion is "a matter of private belief and of conduct in private life . . . is becoming less and less tenable" (pp. 19–20). The Christian is implicated in a number of non-Christian institutions and "he is becoming more and more de-Christianised by all sorts of unconscious pressure" (p. 20). Even to the Christian, "a Christian society only becomes acceptable" after all the alternatives have been examined. We might "sink into an apathetic decline," without faith or philosophy, or develop into a "totalitarian democracy," with conformity and regimentation: "To those who can imagine, and are therefore repelled by, such a prospect, one can assert that the only possibility of control and balance is a religious control and balance" (pp. 21–22).

In outlining the essential features of a Christian Society, Eliot analyzes the Christian State, the Christian Community, and the Community of Christians. The State would be Christian because it would be confined to a Christian framework and attempt to act on Christian principles, not because the rulers would necessarily be Christian. They would be confined to a Christian framework "by the temper and traditions of the people which they rule" (p.

25). Although the rulers would not have to be philosophers, they would have to receive a Christian education which would train them to think in Christian categories, though it would not compel belief. What they believed personally would be less important than the Christian beliefs "to which they would be obliged to conform" (*ICS*, p. 26).

The Christian Community would have little capacity for thinking about the objects of faith; therefore, their Christianity should be confined primarily to behavior (as in their religious observances and their code of behavior toward their neighbors). Their religious and social life ought to form a natural whole, "so that the difficulty of behaving as Christians should not impose an intolerable strain" (*ICS*, p. 27). The parish, subject to modification, would be the community unit. Although Eliot believes that urbanisation is causing the decay of the parish, he takes the parish as a norm or ideal example; for organized community units would have to be created in the Christian State, units to which people would feel attached, making no distinction between the social and religious aspects of their lives.

In setting up the parish as the ideal, as the "community small enough to consist of a nexus of direct personal relationships" (*ICS*, p. 30) Eliot says that he is not advocating that Christians adapt themselves to the status quo. He distinguishes between two types of evil: the evil inherent in human nature and the evil in particular institutions at particular times and places. A Christian Society must face "such problems as the hypertrophy of the motive of Profit into a social ideal, the distinction between the *use* of natural resources and their exploitation, the advantages unfairly accruing to the trader in contrast to the primary producer, the misdirection of the financial machine, the iniquity of usury, and other features of a commercialized society which must be scrutinized on Christian principles" (p. 32). But Eliot maintains that an examination of these problems would distract him from his main purpose, a definition of the end to be attained: "the virtue and well-being in community" and "beatitude—for those who have the eyes to see it" (p. 33).

Since the rulers would be governed by the need to conform, and the Christian Community by custom, the vitality of the Christian Society would depend on the Community of Christians, "the consciously and thoughtfully practicing Christians, especially those of intellectual and spiritual superiority" (*ICS*, p. 34). Eliot differentiates his Community of Christians from Coleridge's "clerisy," which includes the universities, the parochial pastorate, and the local schoolmasters. Eliot's Community of Christians would include members of the laity and clergy who have "superior intellectual and/or spiritual gifts" (p. 37).

The Christian Society must "have a certain uniformity of culture, expressed in education by a settled, though not rigid, agreement as to what everyone should know to some degree, and a positive distinction—however undemocratic it may sound—between the educated and the uneducated" (*ICS*, p. 41). The Community of Christians would have the responsibility of creating "a common system of education and a common culture, which will enable them to influence and be influenced by each other, and collectively to form the conscious mind and the conscience of the nation" (p. 43).

After describing the nature of the Community of Christians, Eliot attempts to define the relation between Church and State in the Christian Society. He recommends, even for countries like the United States, a National Church, in which "dissentients must remain marginal, tending to make only marginal contributions" (*ICS*, p. 46). The Church would have a close relationship to the State, the Christian Community, and the Community of Christians: "a hierarchical organisation in direct and official relation to the State" (p. 47), "a parochial system, in direct contact with the smallest units of the community and their individual members," and through "its masters of ascetic theology and its men of wider interests, a relation to the Community of Christians." The Church in matters of dogma, faith, and morals, "will speak as the final authority" (p. 48), and will criticize the State and be criticized by the Community of Christians.

The idea of a National Church should be balanced by the idea of a Universal Church. The National Church is constantly in danger of being no more than the voice of a "people's prejudice, passion or interest" (*ICS*, p. 55). The allegiance of the individual should be "to the State and to the Church, to one's countrymen and to one's fellow-Christians everywhere, and the latter would always have the primacy. There would always be a tension; and this tension is essential to the idea of a Christian society, and is a distinguishing mark between a Christian and a pagan society" (p. 56).

Eliot maintains that a particular political form should not be identified with Christianity, that the political form is "relative to the character and the stage of intelligence and education of a particular people in a particular place at a particular time" (*ICS*, pp. 57–58). He says that he is not concerned with the differences between economic and

political theories, but with "the more profound differences
between pagan and Christian society" (p. 58). He believes
that preoccupation with politics, particularly foreign affairs, has induced complacency rather than self-examina-
tion. Even concern for the health of the nation is motivated
by fear or jealousy of foreign success; and Christianity is
advocated not because it is true, but because it might be
beneficial.

Eliot does not think that the realization of his ideal
would bring about "a golden age of virtue" (*ICS*, p. 60).
Any human society has its limitations and weaknesses, and
a Christian Society would be no exception. But he thinks
that it would bring about a respect for the religious life
and help man to live in conformity with nature and to
establish a basic philosophy of life, "a pattern into which
all problems of life can have their place." A Christian
Society is the only alternative to a materialistic society: "If
you will not have God (and He is a jealous God) you should
pay your respects to Hitler or Stalin" (p. 64).

Eliot's religious "control and balance," in spite of minor
concessions, are very nearly total: statesmen and teachers
would be forced to conform to Christian dogma, and dissentients would be held to a minimum. The people of his
Ideal Society would simply follow the principles set forth
by the Church or the State or the Community of Christians. Eliot defends his failure to discuss the just society by
maintaining that justice is secondary to the Christian character of the society. Whatever reforms were required
would be required not because they improved people's
lives but because they coincided with Christian doctrine.
He has no faith in the possibility of defining democracy,

saying that the British Fascist General J. F. C. Fuller "has as good a title to call himself a 'believer in democracy' as anyone else" (*ICS*, p. 69).

Eliot points out some of the weaknesses of English and American societies—the dominance of the profit motive, preoccupation with material goods, the shallowness of intellectual life—but he shows little interest in improving these societies. The positive ethics of the Judeo-Christian tradition, the vision of an equalitarian and communal world, drops away, and we are left with a hermetic world of Christian dogma. What attracts Eliot in Christianity is its Pauline characteristics—its unconcern with this world in favor of a promise of the next.

But what is most disturbing in his vision is the quality of life that he imagines for the vast majority of people:

For the great mass of humanity whose attention is occupied mostly by their direct relation to the soil, or the sea, or the machine, and to a small number of persons, pleasures and duties, two conditions are required. The first is that, as their capacity for *thinking* about the objects of faith is small, their Christianity may be almost wholly realised in behavior: both in their customary and periodic religious observances, and in a traditional code of behaviour towards their neighbours. The second is that, while they should have some perception of how far their lives fall short of Christian ideals, their religious and social life should form for them a natural whole, so that the difficulty of behaving as Christians should not impose an intolerable strain. [*ICS*, p. 27]

Whatever Eliot's intentions, the society that he envisions is conformist and repressive. If people have little capacity for thinking, then their lives must be controlled by the Church or the State. Eliot rejects the ideal of equality and diversity, the ideal that everyone, regardless of his beliefs, should fulfill himself in a creative way. He states in *After Strange Gods*, "What is still more important [than homogeneity of culture] is unity of religious background; and reasons of race and religion combine to make any large number of free-thinking Jews undesirable" (pp. 19–20). It is possible that some of the members of the Community of Christians would desire such a society, but what its attractions are for others are not clear.

One might argue that we should not take seriously a vision that is so repressive, that promises so little to the "mass of humanity." In fact, however, although Eliot's social ideas have had much less influence than his literary ideas, they do get a wide hearing, and his concern with religion and spirituality may obscure the basic authoritarianism of his position. Eliot never discusses the enforcing of controls in his proposed society except to imply that the social pressure to conform would be considerable. But one may ask what would happen to the freethinkers (Jews and non-Jews alike) who were regarded as undesirable, and one wonders about the dissenters who would be relegated to a marginal status (*ICS*, p. 46). Eliot seems to believe that his religious objective—"virtue" in community and "beatitude" for some—justifies authoritarianism. At the same time he must have been aware of his appeal to expediency in contending that his proposed society, whatever its disadvantages, would be preferable to socialism or fascism.

Eliot does not attempt to define fascism or socialism or democracy. He merely states that Germany (in the thirties) and the Soviet Union are pagan, without examining their political and economic structures, and that England and the United States have no more right than Nazi Germany to call themselves democracies. This type of argument, which avoids discussing the points it raises, obscures rather than clarifies the issues, as in Eliot's contention that General Fuller has a right to call himself a "believer in democracy." By 1939 the nature of fascism had been well established, and Eliot could have seen for himself whether it satisfied the traditional definition of democracy (a term which, though often loosely used, is not impossible to define). But as he himself says, Eliot is not interested in democracy. The society he envisions is organized hierarchically and controlled by a clerical State.

Eliot's Concept of Culture

Eliot's *Notes towards the Definition of Culture* is a defense of his idea of Christian culture, based on the assumption "that no culture has appeared or developed except together with religion."[3] He combines defense of religion with defense of a stratified society based on wealth and privilege. If the reader "finds it shocking that culture and equalitarianism should conflict, if it seems monstrous to him that anyone should have 'advantages of birth'—I do not ask him to change his faith, I merely ask him to stop paying lip-service to culture" (*NDC*, pp. 14–15).

The term "culture," according to Eliot, has three different associations: relating to the individual, the class, and society. Eliot interprets Arnold's "Culture and Anarchy" as a study concentrating on the perfection of the individual—in the arts, philosophy, and manners. The notion of perfection, however, should "take all three senses of 'culture' into account at once" (*NDC*, p. 22). Although we cannot control culture directly, Eliot believes that we should be concerned with the conditions that contribute to its growth.

Without religion "no culture can appear or develop" (*NDC*, p. 26). Culture is, in fact, "the incarnation . . . of the religion of a people" (p. 27). Culture depends on the development of religion; and the preservation and maintenance of religion depends on the preservation and maintenance of culture: "To judge a work of art by artistic or by religious standards, to judge a religion by religious or artistic standards should come in the end to the same thing: though it is an end at which no individual can arrive" (p. 29). Culture and religion are at the same time identical and separate, involving "all the characteristic activities and interests of a people" (p. 30), including what has been borrowed from primitive peoples. Religion (Christian or non-Christian) "gives an apparent meaning to life, provides the framework for a culture, and protects the mass of humanity from boredom and despair" (p. 32).

Eliot criticizes Karl Mannheim for equating elites and classes and for being concerned only with elites rather than *an* elite (the integration of all elites). The isolation of elites (political, philosophical, artistic, and scientific) should be overcome by a general circulation of ideas and by mutual influences, so that the scientist would be conversant with art, and the artist with science; thus, elites would constitute *the* elite. Eliot argues that although the elites in a class society are usually drawn from the dominant class (the "upper middle class"), they are not the same as that class. To be a member of the upper class requires status and power, but to be a member of an elite requires talent.

The elite, the producers of thought and art, and the

dominant class, the primary consumers of thought and
art, are responsible for the transmission of culture (which
constitutes the way of life of a people). What would happen in a classless society can only be a matter of conjec-
ture. In an optimistic view, the most capable people—in
government, art, science, etc.—would rise to the top. But
even if this occurred, the members of the elite would have
only the common bond of professional interest, "with no
social cohesion, with no social continuity" (*NDC*, p. 46).
Therefore, a society with a class structure is more condu-
cive to culture, for classes imply tradition and the transmission of culture from generation to generation. Although
the existence of classes and elites does not assure the higher
civilization, "when they are absent, the higher civilization is
unlikely to be found" (p. 48).

A flourishing culture will be "neither too united nor too
divided" (*NDC*, p. 49); it will possess both unity and diversity. Not only should there be class culture but also re-
gional culture, which involves loyalties to a particular
place: "each area should have its characteristic culture,
which should also harmonize with, and enrich, the cultures
of the neighbouring areas" (p. 53). For example, the Welsh,
Scottish, and Irish cultures enrich English culture and are
enriched by it.

In addition to geographical unity and diversity of culture, there are also unity and diversity of religion as exemplified in the separation between Protestantism and
Catholicism and the divisions brought about by the various
sects of Protestantism: "We must take note of whatever
injury appears to have been done to European culture, and
to the culture of any part of Europe, by division into sects.
On the other hand, we must acknowledge that many of

the most remarkable achievements of culture have been made since the sixteenth century, in conditions of dis-unity" (*NDC*, p. 71). Anglicanism constitutes a subculture of Latin Europe; and the Protestant sects constitute sec-ondary subcultures. The ideal situation for the main cul-ture, the subculture, and the secondary subcultures is a "constant struggle between the centripetal and centrifugal forces. . . . The local temperament must express its particu-larity in its form of Christianity, and so must the social stratum, so that the culture proper to each area and each class may flourish; but there must also be a force holding these areas and these classes together" (p. 83).

In a stratified society "public affairs would be a respon-sibility not equally borne: a greater responsibility would be inherited by those who inherited special advantages, and in whom self-interest, and interest for the sake of their families ('a stake in the country') should cohere with public spirit. The governing elite, of the nation as a whole, would consist of those whose responsibility was inherited with their affluence and position, and whose forces were con-stantly increased, and often led, by rising individuals of exceptional talents" (*NDC*, p. 85).

The culture-consciousness of our times has "led us to study the relations of imperial powers and subject peoples with a new attention." In controlling other peoples, the imperial nations have become increasingly aware of the importance of cultural differences. Germany, for example, in preparing for war, used culture-consciousness "as a means of uniting a nation against other nations" (*NDC*, p. 91). Britain's rule of India, however, was seldom concerned with culture and proceeded according to a pragmatic philosophy. The British rulers brought to India the so-called advantages of Western Culture but in the process broke up "the native culture on its highest level, without penetrating the mass" (p. 92). Britain had a choice between the imposition of external rule and cultural assimilation. "The failure to arrive at the latter is a religious failure." If the British had recognized the importance of religion in the formation of their own culture, they could have recognized and paid attention to its importance in the preservation of Indian culture. We should not conclude, however, that the "damage that has been done to native cultures in the process of imperial expansion is . . . an indictment of empire itself" (p. 93).

In his analysis of the relationship of culture to education, Eliot examines the various assumptions of the nature of education. The first assumption is that any discussion of education requires that the purpose of education be stated, a different task from defining the word "education." According to the definition given by the Oxford dictionary, which Eliot cites, education is (1) "the process of bringing up (young persons)"; (2) "the systematic instruction, schooling or training given to the young (and, by extension, to adults) in preparation for the work of life"; and (3) "culture or development of powers, formation of character" (*NDC*, p. 97). Eliot comments that whereas the dictionary is merely stating the various assumptions (in different historical periods) about the nature of education, those who discuss the purpose of education are concerned either with what they believe to be the unconscious purpose or with their opinion of what the purpose should be. For example, in *The Churches Survey Their Task* (1937) the purpose is stated as the transmission of culture.

Other views of the purposes of education are the in-

culcation of democracy, professional training, and the
achievement of happiness. C. E. M. Joad (in *About Education*) states three purposes: the earning of a living, citizenship, and the development of latent powers. But each of
these purposes, Eliot says, needs qualification. The development of a person's latent powers might impair his ability
to make a living; education for citizenship in a democracy
is not an essential purpose but a pragmatic one, which
could be applied by any society (democratic or despotic);
and finally the development of latent powers is too much
to hope for, depending on too many variables. In contrast
to these purposes, Eliot proposes acquisition of wisdom,
satisfaction of curiosity, and respect for learning.

Eliot takes exception to three other current assumptions:
that education makes people happier, that everyone wants
an education, and that education should be organized so
as to provide equality of opportunity. There is no evidence,
Eliot argues, that the educated are happier than the uneducated, although the uneducated may believe that education would raise their standard of living or that they
have been denied something that would have made them
happier. But education above one's social level or above
one's abilities may produce unhappiness. Furthermore, if
education were imposed on everyone, many would react
with hostility: "A high average of general education is perhaps less necessary for a civil society than is a respect for
learning."

Education "should help to preserve the class and to
select the élite," and "the exceptional individual should
have the opportunity to elevate himself in the social scale."
On the other hand, our ideal should not be "an educational
system which would automatically sort out everyone ac-

cording to his native capacities," for such a system "would disorganize society, by substituting for classes, élites of brains." Education would be restricted to "what will lead to success in the world," and success would be restricted "to those persons who have been good pupils of the system" (*NDC*, p. 103). The ideal society includes the privilege of class, which assures tradition and an established way of life.

Eliot's ideal is in direct opposition to that of Arnold, for Arnold conceives of an equalitarian culture which "seeks to do away with classes; to make the best that has been thought and known in the world current everywhere."[4] Culture raises the whole level of society, enabling each individual to realize his full potentialities. Arnold, in fact, makes equality of opportunity a condition of culture. Not only does the individual realize his best self and experience the development of all the qualities that contribute to his happiness, but he lives in a society that promotes this development. Arnold's ideal is spiritual perfection, which supersedes all narrow goals, such as wealth or "right action" or political democracy (all constituting the "machinery" of society).

Eliot's concept of culture, of a society in which there is conflict between the parts but no change, fits well with his philosophy of resignation, which he opposes to the Romantic philosophy of aspiration. His comments on society are not attempts at analysis but subjective projections, statements of his own "feelings and perhaps of a few of his more sympathetic readers" (*NDC*, p. 111); these are exemplified in his statement that Britain's damage to Indian culture should not be regarded as a condemnation of empire (p. 93) or that we would be unhappy in a future society, even though we were ignorant of the nature of that society (p. 16). Eliot follows the advice he gives in *After Strange Gods:* he simply asserts the point of view that a stratified and authoritarian society provides the only grounds for the advancement of culture.

[VI]

CONCLUSION

ALTHOUGH Eliot opposes the idea of direct personal expression, he bases his theory of poetry on the idea of
indirect personal expression. According to Eliot, the poet
begins with his own emotion and "escapes" it in the creative process of writing a poem, but at the same time expresses his emotion indirectly by creating an objective
structure that embodies the particular emotions expe-
rienced by the character or characters represented. The
poet's emotion is not in the poem but is implied by the pattern of the characters' action (SE, p. 173). The reader responds ideally with an art emotion, evoked by the esthetic
quality of the work.

The early Eliot judges esthetic quality according to the
degree of the poem's emotional intensity, which is dependent on the interaction of situation (structural emotion)
and images (feelings). This interaction produces the neces-

sary conditions for an art emotion. The structural emotion is related to the dramatic situation, which motivates the emotion of the character, and is represented (or "expressed") by a series of images.

Eliot's concept of the objective correlative, the causative situation related to the structural emotion, is usually interpreted to mean an image or situation or poem which expresses the poet's emotion. Although Eliot holds that images express emotions and that the work corresponds to the poet's emotion, the objective correlative refers (as has been earlier stressed) to the situation in the work that motivates the character's emotion—such as Gertrude's over-hasty marriage in *Hamlet* or Lady Macbeth's involvement in Duncan's murder. The emphasis is on situation or plot as a cause of emotion, rather than on images as an expression of emotion.

Intensity is not achieved, however, until images are combined with the situation. All poetry, Eliot says (1921), is characterized by "a degree of heterogeneity of material compelled into unity by the operation of the poet's mind" (*SE*, p. 243). Eliot paraphrases Johnson's description of Metaphysical poetry as "the most heterogeneous ideas . . . yoked by violence together" but substitutes "unity" for "yoked." In effect, Eliot states that all poetry has some similarity to Metaphysical poetry—"heterogeneity . . . compelled into unity"—a concept similar to Coleridge's "reconcilement of opposite or discordant qualities." But when Eliot examines Metaphysical poetry, he finds, like Johnson, that it differs from other types of poetry, that it is characterized by an integration of wit and emotion, a quality that contemporary poetry (1921) lacks. As he says in his essay on Andrew Marvell, Eliot prefers poetry that combines wit and seriousness. He shifts his view from poetry in general to Metaphysical poetry, which involves a special reconcilement, or combination, of wit and emotion. He moves from "heterogeneity of material" (his modification of Johnson's "heterogeneous ideas") to the balance or reconcilement of opposed attitudes.

The combination of wit and emotion constitutes the basis of Eliot's concept of the dissociation of sensibility. Eliot maintains that the Metaphysical poets were able to achieve an integration of idea and image, of wit and emotion, and of language and sensibility, and that in the seventeenth century, just after the Metaphysicals, this integration was impaired or dissociated—as in the works of Dryden and Milton. Although agreeing with Coleridge that all poetry is characterized by diversity in unity, Eliot states his preference for that poetry which represents a unified sensibility—the integration of idea and image, of wit and emotion, and of language and sensibility.

The phrase "dissociation of sensibility," after being interpreted as a split between emotion (religion) and reason (science), became highly influential in criticism, constituting, for example, the basis of Basil Willey's *The Seventeenth Century Background* (1934). As Frank Kermode points out in *Romantic Image* (1957), numerous critics have taken for granted that a dissociation between religious emotion and philosophical or scientific reason occurred sometime during the Renaissance and damaged the poetic tradition, with the result that poetry became either imagistic or abstract. But Eliot's "dissociation of sensibility" does not refer to a split between religious emotion and abstract or scientific reason. He is primarily concerned with the loss of intellectuality or wit, the substitution of sentimentality or "rumination" for the integration of wit and emotion.

Eliot attempts in his early criticism to judge intensity in poetry on wholly esthetic grounds, saying that the philosophical belief expressed by the poem, or held by the poet, should not affect the evaluation of the poem. He maintained for a brief time that belief is wholly integrated into the reality of the poem and cannot be separated from this reality. In the middle twenties, however, he tentatively accepted I. A. Richards' principle of pseudo-statements, the theory that the ideas of the poem evoke neither belief nor disbelief but satisfy the emotional needs of the reader. But in the late twenties he stated that we are likely to gain more pleasure from those poems which express beliefs with which we agree. He finally concludes that we should judge a poem both by its literary merits and the quality of the philosophy it expresses or implies.

Eliot's early theory of criticism is that we should evaluate the work "according to [esthetic] standards, in comparison to other works" (SE, p. 122). He is sceptical of the effectiveness of interpretation, showing a practitioner's interest in technique, particularly in poetic style or imagery, and his best critical practice is in the examination and comparison of lines or passages of poetry (as exemplified by his essay on Andrew Marvell). In itself, however, the method of analysis does not guarantee the "sense of fact" (SE, p. 19) that Eliot desires in criticism, for analysis (the detailed evaluation of esthetic qualities) is as subject to error as interpretation. In his scepticism toward interpretation, Eliot may be partially responsible for the concept that evaluative analysis, judging "according to standards," is the true function of criticism and that the attempt to determine meaning is a violation of the work's artistic integrity.

Eliot becomes in the thirties a moral pragmatist, judging the work according to its effect on the reader. He does not abandon his theory that the work is an emotional structure, but he becomes primarily concerned with the moral and religious qualities of literature, showing more interest in social and religious criticism than in literary criticism. In *After Strange Gods, The Idea of a Christian Society,* and *Notes towards the Definition of Culture* he sets forth his views on the need for a stratified society dominated by a national church.

Eliot's social ideas are in the tradition established by the early twentieth-century poet and critic, T. E. Hulme, who based his criticism on the concept of original sin, arguing that man needs order and discipline—"classicism" as opposed to "romanticism." Since man, in Eliot's view, is basically evil, he requires a strong religious authority that can discipline him and curb his individualistic desires. Whatever Eliot's intentions and whatever the extent of his religious justifications, his authoritarianism supports an elitist society which protects and advances the interests of a minority.

Eliot's influence on literary criticism is confined mostly to his early work as an analytical critic. The revolt of the twenties against literary history, against a concern with background and biography, was aided by *The Sacred Wood* (1920), which seemed to define what the function of the critic should be—concentration on poetry as art. Eliot's theory of impersonality, his rejection of the idea of direct personal expression, provided support for the contextualist view that the poem is an independent verbal structure. His interest in esthetic analysis, in the integration of idea and image, and in a poetry of complexity parallels some of the major concerns of the contextualist movement. Eliot's criticism is not concerned, however, with the close reading of texts, with the explication of meaning, which is really a problem of interpretation. His criticism is "close" only in the sense that the esthetic analyses in some of his early essays are detailed. He felt that evaluation should concentrate on the actual words and lines of the poem, and he deplored vague appreciations. It is in this insistence, in his early essays, on detailed esthetic analysis that his influence on criticism has been strongest.

Notes

CHAPTER I: THE CRITICAL STANDARD

1. *Selected Essays*, 2nd ed. (New York, 1950), pp. 4–5—hereafter cited as *SE*.

2. *The Sacred Wood*, 7th ed. (London, 1950), pp. xv–xvi—hereafter cited as *SW*.

3. *After Strange Gods* (London, 1934), pp. 18, 29.

4. F. O. Matthiessen, *The Achievement of T. S. Eliot*, 3rd ed. (New York and London, 1958), p. 7.

5. Introduction to *Le Serpent*, by Paul Valéry, trans. Mark Wardle (London, 1924), p. 12.

6. Sister Mary Costello, in a study of Eliot's concept of poetry, concludes that Eliot bases his definition of poetry on the emotional intensity of language (*Between Fixity and Flux* [Washington, D.C., 1947]).

7. "Prose and Verse," *Chapbook*, no. 22 (April 1921), p. 6.

8. "The Three Voices of Poetry," in *On Poetry and Poets*, Noonday ed. (New York, 1961), p. 107.

9. Introduction to *Selected Poems by Marianne Moore*, ed. T. S. Eliot (New York, 1935), p. xi.

10. Introduction to *Ezra Pound, Selected Poems*, ed. T. S. Eliot (London, 1928), p. 16. Ants Oras, basing his analysis on "Tradition and the Individual Talent" and Eliot's introduction

to Pound's poetry, gives an account of Eliot's concept of the creative process in *The Critical Ideas of T. S. Eliot* (Tartu, U.S.S.R., 1932), pp. 12–13.

11. *John Dryden: the Poet, the Dramatist, the Critic* (New York, 1932), p. 32.

12. As quoted by M. H. Abrams, *The Mirror and the Lamp* (New York, 1953), pp. 241, 145.

13. René Wellek and Austin Warren, *Theory of Literature* (New York, 1949), p. 73.

14. The integral relationship between meaning and author is persuasively argued by E. D. Hirsch, Jr., in "Objective Interpretation," *PMLA* 75 (Sept. 1960): 463–79, and by Leon Edel, in *Literary Biography* (New York, 1959), who also maintains that the relationship between biography and text plays a role in the evaluation of a work. Hirsch expands his argument in *Validity in Interpretation* (New Haven and London, 1967).

15. "John Milton," *English Institute Essays 1946* (New York, 1947), p. 15. Edel applies Bush's statement to Samson's blindness (*Literary Biography*, p. 62).

16. "The Music of Poetry," in *On Poetry and Poets*, p. 22.

17. *The Use of Poetry and the Use of Criticism* (London, 1933), p. 35—hereafter cited as *UP*.

18. I. A. Richards argues that we cannot "postulate a peculiar" esthetic value, "different in kind and cut off from the other values of ordinary experiences" (*Principles of Literary Criticism* [London, 1925], p. 17).

19. "Poetry and Propaganda," *Bookman* 70 (Feb. 1930): 599.

CHAPTER II: THE INTENSITY OF POETRY

1. Eliot's concept of the poet's mind as a "receptacle" of images may have been influenced by Rémy de Gourmont, who maintains that artistic creation is impossible without "a reservoir of images," from which the imagination creates new and

infinite combinations (*Le Problème du Style*, 9th ed. [Paris, 1902], p. 35).

2. Introduction to *Ezra Pound, Selected Poems*, ed. T. S. Eliot (London, 1928), p. 16.

3. "Reflections on Contemporary Poetry," *Egoist* 4 (Sept. 1917): 118.

4. Introduction to *Selected Poems by Marianne Moore*, ed. T. S. Eliot (New York, 1935), p. xi.

5. Preface to *Anabasis*, by St.-J.Perse, trans. T. S. Eliot (London, 1930), p. 8.

6. For the various concepts which may be included under the heading of "objective correlative," see Robert Stallman's *The Critic's Notebook* (Minneapolis and London, 1950), pp. 115–74. Stallman's book includes a quotation from Washington Allston (*Lectures on Art*, 1850), who was evidently the first to use the term. Allston's term means any material object—natural or artificial—which is a correlative of the Platonic Idea pre-existing in the mind. Allston probably owes his term to Coleridge's "necessary correlative of object," which refers to the relationship between mental image and object (*Biographia Literaria*, ed. J. Shawcross [London, 1962], I: 174). Bernard Bosanquet uses the phrase the "connecting and pervading correlations" of feeling in *Three Lectures on Aesthetic* (London, 1915), p. 19. As Sister Mary Costello points out, Whitman speaks in the preface to *Leaves of Grass* of the poet's matching of "every thought or act by its correlative." Another analogue, noted by John M. Steadman in *Notes and Queries* 5 (June 1958): 261–62, is Edmund Husserl's "Objektives Korrelat," first used in 1900 in *Logische Untersuchungen*. The meaning of Eliot's term, as René Wellek maintains, is remote from Pound's concept of poetry as equations for the human emotions ("Criticism of T. S. Eliot," *Sewanee Review* 64 [Summer 1956]: 418).

7. F. O. Matthiessen, *The Achievement of T. S. Eliot*, 3rd ed. (New York and London, 1958), pp. 58, 62, 64–65; Eliseo

Vivas, "The Objective Correlative of T. S. Eliot," in *Critiques and Essays in Criticism,* ed. Robert Stallman (New York, 1949), p. 396.

8. René Wellek makes a similar point: "Apparently Eliot means that Hamlet's disgust with life (which seems very well expressed) is not fully motivated by the marriage of his mother and the suspected murder of his father" ("Criticism of Eliot," p. 419). William K. Wimsatt, Jr., and Monroe C. Beardsley argue that "Hamlet's emotion must be expressible . . . and actually expressed too (by something) in the play; otherwise . . . Eliot would not know it is there—in excess of the facts" ("The Affective Fallacy," in *Critiques and Essays in Criticism,* pp. 407–408).

9. Wellek's interpretation of the correlative as a "symbolic structure" between poet and reader is similarly disproved ("Criticism of Eliot," p. 420).

10. *Dictionary of World Literature,* s.v., "Objective Correlative."

11. Robert Stallman, "The New Critics," in *Critiques and Essays in Criticism,* p. 502.

12. David L. Stevenson uses the term in this sense in "An Objective Correlative for T. S. Eliot's Hamlet," *Journal of Aesthetics and Art Criticism* 13 (Sept. 1954): 69–79. Stevenson, who is concerned primarily with the argument that Hamlet is motivated, assumes that there is no question about the meaning of "objective correlative."

13. Wimsatt and Beardsley, "Affective Fallacy," p. 409. In the discussion the authors employ the term "objective correlative" for their own purposes—an image correlative to the literal reason for emotion.

14. Eliot's concept of the objective correlative may have been influenced by Irving Babbitt's idea of the "disproportion" between the "outer incident" and the emotion of the "Rousseauist" (*Rousseau and Romanticism* [New York, 1955], p. 172).

15. F. W. Bateson, "Contributions to a Dictionary of Critical Terms," *Essays in Criticism* 1 (July 1951): 302–12; Basil Willey, *The Seventeenth Century Background* (London, 1934), pp. 87–88, 205–206, 291–95.

16. Frank Kermode, *Romantic Image* (New York, 1957), pp. 138–61.

17. W. K. Wimsatt and Cleanth Brooks, *Literary Criticism, A Short History* (New York, 1957), p. 284.

CHAPTER III: POETRY AND BELIEF

1. Victor Brombert bases a Yale undergraduate honors study, *The Criticism of T. S. Eliot: Problems of an "Impersonal Theory" of Poetry* (New Haven, 1949), on Eliot's shift from an "esthetic" to a "religious-esthetic" standard. William Joseph Rooney in *The Problem of "Poetry and Belief" in Contemporary Criticism* (Washington, D.C., 1949) concentrates on Eliot's opinions during the late twenties, concluding that "Eliot offers a set of general propositions for the solution of the problem [of belief], propositions which seem to him to be sound; but in applying these principles he finds that difficulties of sufficient weight and intractability arise to force him to the conclusion that his experience does not verify the general propositions he has offered and thinks valid [that belief does not affect our evaluation of a poem]" (pp. 99–100).

2. "Kipling Redivivus," *Athenaeum*, 9 May 1919, p. 298.

3. "A Note on Poetry and Belief," *Enemy* 1 (Jan. 1927): 15–16.

4. "Literature, Science and Dogma," *Dial* 82 (Mar. 1927): 241.

5. "Milton I," in *On Poetry and Poets*, Noonday ed. (New York, 1961), p. 56.

6. "Experiment in Criticism," *Bookman* 70 (Nov. 1929): 226.

7. "Poetry and Propaganda," *Bookman* 70 (Feb. 1930): 601.

8. Cleanth Brooks, *The Well Wrought Urn: Studies in the Structure of Poetry* (New York, 1947), p. 228; René Wellek, "Criticism of T. S. Eliot," *Sewanee Review* 64 (Summer 1956): 416.

9. M. H. Abrams, "Belief and the Suspension of Disbelief," in *Literature and Belief*, ed. M. H. Abrams (New York, 1958), pp. 5–6.

10. Murray Krieger, *The New Apologists for Poetry* (Minneapolis, 1956), p. 22.

11. Cleanth Brooks, "Implications of an Organic Theory of Poetry," in *Literature and Belief*, p. 68.

CHAPTER IV: THE CRITICAL PRACTICE

1. "Studies in Contemporary Criticism," *Egoist* 5 (Oct. 1918): 113.

2. Introduction to *The Wheel of Fire*, by G. Wilson Knight (London, 1930), p. xv.

3. Introduction to *Ezra Pound, Selected Poems*, ed. T. S. Eliot (London, 1928), p. xi.

4. "American Literature," *Athenaeum*, 25 April 1919, p. 237.

5. *After Strange Gods* (London, 1934), p. 13.

6. M. C. Bradbrook, "Eliot's Critical Method," in *T. S. Eliot: A Study of His Writings by Several Hands*, ed. B. Rajan (New York, 1964), p. 125.

7. *John Dryden: the Poet, the Dramatist, the Critic* (New York, 1932), p. 55.

8. "A Review of John Murray's Shakespeare," *Criterion* 15 (July 1936): 708; "The Music of Poetry," in *On Poetry and Poets*, Noonday ed. (New York, 1961), p. 18. The other statement on this issue appears in "Milton II," in *On Poetry and Poets*, p. 167.

9. "Views and Reviews," *New English Weekly* 7 (June 1935): 190.

10. "Reflections on Vers Libre," *New Statesman* 8 (Mar. 1917): 519.

11. Stanley Hyman, *The Armed Vision* (New York, 1948), p. 76.

12. "The Music of Poetry," in *On Poetry and Poets*, p. 17.

13. See Tucker Brooke, *A Literary History of England*, ed. Albert Baugh (New York, 1948), p. 515.

CHAPTER V: THE SOCIAL CRITICISM

1. *After Strange Gods* (London, 1934), p. 13. Hereafter referred to in the text as *ASG*.

2. *The Idea of a Christian Society* (New York, 1940), p. 6. Hereafter referred to in the text as *ICS*.

3. *Notes towards the Definition of Culture* (New York, 1949), p. 13. Hereafter referred to in the text as *NDC*.

4. Matthew Arnold, *Culture and Anarchy, with Friendship's Garland and Some Literary Essays*, ed. R. H. Super (Ann Arbor, Mich., 1965), p. 113.

An Annotated Bibliography

This bibliography is arranged chronologically and includes all of Eliot's books on criticism, all articles that he collected in book form, and what I consider his most significant articles (in periodicals) and introductions to books. For a general listing, consult Donald Gallup's *T. S. Eliot: A Bibliography,* 2nd ed. (New York, 1969).

Review of *Theism and Humanism,* by the Rt. Hon. A. J. Balfour. *International Journal of Ethics* 26 (Jan. 1916): 284–89. This is a brilliant book, "a protest against the aesthetics, the ethics, and the epistemology of 'Naturalism.'" The basic argument is that theism alone can explain the existence of value and of truth. The weakness of the book is that it fails to distinguish between value and belief about value and between truth and true belief. Mr. Balfour presents his own case persuasively, but his attack on science or materialist philosophy is unconvincing.

"The Borderline of Prose." *New Statesman* 9 (May 1917): 157–59. The only absolute distinction to be drawn between poetry and prose "is that poetry is written in verse, and prose is written in prose; or, in other words, that there is prose rhythm and verse rhythm." When we use the terms "poetic" or "prosaic," we refer to some quality which may exist in either verse or prose. "The distinction between poetry and prose must be a technical distinction; and future refinement of both poetry and prose can only draw the distinction more clearly."

"Reflections on Contemporary Poetry (I)." *Egoist* 4 (Sept. 1917): 118–19. One of the ways by which contemporary poetry has tried to escape the rhetorical, the abstract, the moralized, "to recover (for that is its purpose) the accents of direct speech, is to concentrate its attention upon trivial or accidental or commonplace objects." Contemporary American poetry concentrates on the accidental, whereas contemporary English poetry concentrates on the trivial. The latter tendency is Wordsworthian—"the emotion is of the object and not of human life." The ideal, achieved by John Donne, is to employ objects to express emotions which are "definitely human."

Ezra Pound, His Metric and Poetry. New York, 1917. Pound's verse reveals an adaptation of meter to mood. It "is always definite and concrete because he has always a definite emotion behind it."

"In Memory of Henry James." *Egoist* 5 (Jan 1918): 1–2. Reprinted in *Little Review* 5 (Aug. 1918): 44–47. Henry James "had a mind so fine that no idea could violate it." Most of us "corrupt our feelings with ideas; we produce the public, the political, the emotional idea, evading sensation and thought." James maintains a "point of view, a view-point untouched by the parasite idea."

"Studies in Contemporary Criticism." *Egoist* 5 (Oct. 1918): 113–14. "The work of the critic is almost wholly comprehended in the 'complementary activities' of comparison and analysis." His judgment and appreciation should not be stated but implied by the "laboratory work" of comparison and analysis.

"A Brief Treatise on the Criticism of Poetry." *Chapbook,* no. 9 (March 1920), pp. 1–10. The kind of criticism, such as Walter Pater's, that is "etiolated creation" is of no importance. Historical or philosophical criticism, such as Sainte-Beuve's, is not literary but is nevertheless "perfectly legitimate." The third type of criticism is the criticism of poetry proper, such as that of Dryden or Aristotle. "The historical or the philosophical critic of poetry is criticizing poetry in order to create a history or philosophy; the poetic critic is criticizing poetry in order to create poetry." Ideally, the critic of poetry should himself be a poet. The "good critic will merely say 'this is a good poem' in a hundred different ways. He will make a column of it. He will quote and quote." Reviewing and criticism, however, should not be confused. Reviewing "should be done by critics, but critics have other things to do as well." Unfortunately, much reviewing is poor, more commercial than artistic.

The Sacred Wood: Essays on Poetry and Criticism. London, 1920; New York, 1921. 2nd ed., London, 1928; New York, 1930.

Preface (1928). The essays are concerned with the problem of the integrity of poetry (poetry as poetry and not another thing) as opposed to the problem that Eliot says he is now (in 1928 and thereafter) interested in, that of determining the relation of poetry "to the spiritual and social life of its time and other times."

Introduction. Matthew Arnold dissipated his energy in criticizing the uncritical.

"The Perfect Critic." The ideal critic (exemplified by Aristotle) transforms his personal impressions into laws or principles.

"Imperfect Critics." These critics are either appreciators or moralists (includes notes on Swinburne, George Wyndham, Charles Whibley, and Paul Elmer More).

"Tradition and the Individual Talent." The poet achieves impersonality (expressing his personality indirectly) by fitting into tradition and by concentrating on his craft rather than his emotions.

"The Possibility of a Poetic Drama." The problem is to take a form of entertainment and transform it into poetry.

"Euripides and Professor Murray." Murray's translation of Euripides' *Medea* is poor.

" 'Rhetoric' and Poetic Drama." Rhetoric is either speech which reveals a character (as Cyrano) who sees himself as a dramatic figure, or speech which attempts to create an effect of "general impressiveness."

"Notes on the Blank Verse of Christopher Marlowe." Marlowe's style moves in an un-Shakespearean direction, toward "something not unlike caricature."

"Hamlet and His Problems." Hamlet lacks an objective correlative," a sufficient motive for his emotion.

"Ben Jonson." Jonson's poetry is "of the surface" (lacking a "third dimension") but not superficial.

"Philip Massinger." Massinger exemplifies the dissociation between language (refined) and sensibility (crude).

"Swinburne as Poet." It is the word that gives Swinburne the thrill, not the object.

"Blake." Blake is terrifyingly honest, but he suffers from not having a framework of traditional ideas.

"Dante." Dante deals with his philosophy not as "comment or reflection" but as "something *perceived.*"

"Prose and Verse." *Chapbook,* no. 22 (Apr. 1921), pp. 3–10.
"The distinction between 'verse' and 'prose' is clear; the
distinction between 'poetry' and 'prose' is very obscure."
Emotional intensity in the details of the work of art is sometimes said to distinguish poetry from prose. It is true that
great poetry captures and puts into literature an emotion.
On the other hand, poetry and prose cannot be distinguished
on the basis of thinking and feeling. Poetry consists of a
"cumulative succession of images each fusing with the next;
or by the rapid and unexpected combination of images apparently unrelated, which have their relationship enforced
upon them by the mind of the author." But there are not
two distinct faculties, one of imagination (poetry) and one
of reason (prose). The most valuable distinction between
poetry and prose is probably that based on versification.

*Homage to John Dryden: Three Essays on Poetry of the Seven-
teenth Century.* London, 1924.

Preface. Eliot says that he had intended to write a series of
essays on the seventeenth and eighteenth centuries, but
lacked sufficient leisure to do so. He feels that the poetry of
the seventeenth and eighteenth centuries "possesses an ele-
gance and a dignity absent from the popular and pretentious
verse of the Romantic Poets and their successors."
"John Dryden." Dryden, one of our wittiest poets, has the
power of transforming "the prosaic into the poetic, the trivial
into the magnificent."
"The Metaphysical Poets." The Metaphysical poets possess an
integration of wit and emotion, idea and image, and
language and sensibility—an integration lost in later poetry,
creating "a dissociation of sensibility."
"Andrew Marvell." Marvell's poetry possesses concrete imagery
and an integration of wit and emotion.

"A Note on Poetry and Belief." *Enemy,* no. 1 (Feb. 1927), pp.
15–17. I. A. Richards maintains that "The Waste Land"
effects a complete separation between poetry and all beliefs;
but such a separation is impossible. Even doubt or uncer-
tainty is a kind of belief, and what the author believes cannot be separated from what he writes. "It takes application,
and a kind of genius, to believe anything, and to believe
anything (I do *not* mean merely to believe in some 'religion')
will probably become more and more difficult as time goes
on."

For Lancelot Andrewes: Essays on Style and Order. London,
1928; New York, 1929.

Preface. The point of view of the essays "may be described as
classicist in literature, royalist in politics, and anglo-catholic
in religion."
"Lancelot Andrewes." Andrewes's style possesses ordonnance,
precision, and relevant intensity. His sermons are superior
to those of John Donne because "Andrewes is wholly absorbed in the object and therefore responds with the adequate emotion," whereas Donne uses his sermons as a means
of self-expression.
"John Bramhall." Bramhall, Bishop of Derry under Charles I,
argues convincingly against the deterministic materialism of
Thomas Hobbes.
"Niccolo Machiavelli." Machiavelli wrote intelligently on politics, arguing that the church is necessary for order in the
state and that wavering humanity needs a strong government.
"Francis Herbert Bradley." Bradley attacks Arnold's concept
of God as the moral behavior (the best self) of human beings. Bradley wanted "to determine how much of morality
could be founded securely without entering into the religious
questions at all." He was certainly not unaware, however,

that our common-sense knowledge does not in itself go far
enough.

"Baudelaire in Our Time." Baudelaire was "essentially a Christian, born out of his due time, and a classicist, born out of
his due time." He attained the most difficult of Christian
virtues, the virtue of humility.

"Thomas Middleton." Middleton, the most impersonal of
Elizabethan dramatists, is a great poet, portraying the "fundamental passions of any time and any place."

"A Note on Richard Crashaw." Crashaw creates images that
possess "brain work," with a "deliberate conscious perversity
of language," whereas Shelley "keeps his images on one side
and his meanings on the other."

"The Humanism of Irving Babbitt." Babbitt's humanism bears
the same relationship to religion that humanitarianism bears
to humanism: humanitarianism suppresses the human; humanism suppresses the divine. Babbitt's ethics are dependent
ultimately on the individual himself, not on any external
authority, "anterior, exterior, or superior to the individual."
Babbitt apparently wants man to will civilization, but civilization cannot exist without religion.

"Experiment in Criticism." *Bookman* 70 (Nov. 1929): 225–33.
Reprinted in *Literary Opinion in America.* Edited by Morton
Dauwen Zabel. Rev. ed. New York, 1951, pp. 606–17: The
criticism of the seventeenth and eighteenth centuries assumes that literature is something to be enjoyed, whereas
criticism in the nineteenth and twentieth centuries usually
assumes that literature is a "means for eliciting truth or
acquiring knowledge." Coleridge's *Biographia Literaria* (an
"experiment in criticism"), with its application of philosophy
to literature, was important in helping to bring about a
change in perspective. Sainte-Beuve, with his historical approach, also helped to effect a change. The tendency
throughout the modern period "has been to widen the scope

of criticism and increase the demands made upon the critic."
But the first purpose of literature "must always be what it
always has been—to give a peculiar kind of pleasure which
has something constant in it throughout the ages. . . . The
task of criticism will be, accordingly, not only to expand its
borders but to clarify its center."

"Poetry and Propaganda." *Bookman* 70 (Feb. 1930): 595–602.
Reprinted in *Literary Opinion in America*, pp. 97–107: We
can "hardly doubt that the 'truest' philosophy is the best
material for the greatest poet; so that the poet must be rated
in the end both by the philosophy he realizes in poetry and
by the fulness and adequacy of the realization." Poetry "is
not the assertion that something is true, but the making
that truth more fully real to us; it is the creation of a sensuous embodiment." "We aim ideally to come to rest in some
poetry which shall realize poetically what we ourselves believe; but we have no contact with poetry unless we can pass
in and out freely among the various worlds of poetic creation."

Preface to *Anabasis*, by St.-J. Perse. Translated by T. S. Eliot.
London, 1930. The poem is a sequence of images arranged
according to the logic of imagination. Mr. Perse is able "to
write poetry in what is called prose." In discussing the distinction between poetry and prose, "we have three terms
where we need four: we have 'verse' and 'poetry' on the one
side, and only 'prose' on the other." But the logic of *Anabasis'*
imagery is that of poetry, not of prose.

Introduction to *The Wheel of Fire*, by G. Wilson Knight. London, 1930. The attempt to interpret works of art seems to be
something that we are all driven to. But the practitioner of
verse is sceptical of the efficacy of interpretation, limiting
himself to the "analysis of line, metric and cadence." There

is "an essential part of error in all interpretation," for interpretation is dependent on abstractions from the experience of art. If we lived Shakespeare's work completely, "we should need no interpretation; but on our plane of appearances our interpretations themselves are a part of our living."

Selected Essays. London, 1932; New York, 1932; 2nd English ed., London, 1932; 2nd American ed., New York, 1950; 3rd English ed., London, 1951. The dates of six essays in the 1932 edition are in error: "Tradition and the Individual Talent" (1917), "Euripides and Professor Murray" (1918), "Cyril Tourneur" (1931), "John Dryden" (1922), "Francis Herbert Bradley" (1926), and "The Humanism of Irving Babbitt" (1927). All errors, except for the dating of "The Humanism of Irving Babbitt," are corrected in the 1950 American edition; but one new error, "1928" for "1929," for "Second Thoughts about Humanism" occurs. All dates are correct in the third English edition (Donald Gallup, *Bibliography*, p. 48). Four essays from *Essays Ancient and Modern* (1936) are added to the 1950 American edition: "In Memoriam" (1936), "Religion and Literature" (1935), "The Pensées of Pascal" (1931), and "Modern Education and the Classics" (1932). One essay from *Elizabethan Essays* (1934) is added to the 1951 English edition. This is "John Marston" (1934).

Preface to the 3rd English ed. Eliot finds himself inclined to quarrel with his own judgments. The book should be regarded as a kind of historical record of his interests and opinions.

"Tradition and the Individual Talent" (1919).

"The Function of Criticism" (1923). The function of criticism is the "elucidation of works of art and the correction of taste." The basic principles of criticism should be objectivity and a sense of fact.

"'Rhetoric' and Poetic Drama" (1919).

"A Dialogue on Dramatic Poetry" (1928). Good drama requires poetry, not as an embellishment, but as an effective means of representing character and emotion.

"Euripides and Professor Murray" (1920).

"Seneca in Elizabethan Translation" (1927). Although there is a dissociation in Seneca between language and sensibility, much can be "said for Seneca as a dramatist." His influence on the spectacle, language, and thought of Elizabethan drama was extensive.

"Four Elizabethan Dramatists" (Webster, Tourneur, Middleton, and Chapman: 1924). Elizabethan drama should not be judged by the standards of photographic realism, which are obviously inappropriate, but by the standards of convention and poetic value.

"Christopher Marlowe" (a reprint of "Notes on the Blank Verse of Christopher Marlowe" from *The Sacred Wood;* 1919).

"Shakespeare and the Stoicism of Seneca" (1927). Shakespeare reflects, although he did not necessarily believe, the Senecan philosophy of stoic fatalism and self-dramatization.

"Hamlet and His Problems" (1919).

"Ben Jonson" (1919).

"Thomas Middleton" (1927).

"Thomas Heywood" (1931). Heywood "was a facile and sometimes felicitous purveyor of goods to the popular taste."

"Cyril Tourneur" (1930). Tourneur's place as a great poet is assured by *The Revenger's Tragedy,* which expresses, in exactly the right words and rhythms, a "loathing and disgust of humanity."

"John Ford" (1932). Although Ford's poetry is "of the surface," he succeeded in creating a blank verse "which is quite his own."

"Philip Massinger" (1920).

"John Marston" (1934). "It is not by writing quotable 'poetic' passages, but by giving us the sense of something behind, more real than any of his personages and their action, that Marston establishes himself among the writers of genius." His best play is *The Wonder of Women.*

"Dante" (1929). It is not necessary to agree with Dante's philosophy in order to appreciate his poetry, an exemplification of a *visual* imagination; on the other hand, "one probably has more pleasure in the poetry when one shares the beliefs of the poet."

"The Metaphysical Poets" (1921).

"Andrew Marvell" (1921).

"John Dryden" (1921).

"William Blake" (a reprint of "Blake" from *The Sacred Wood;* 1920).

"Swinburne as Poet" (1920).

"In Memoriam" (1936). "In Memoriam" is a profound expression of Tennyson's melancholy.

"Lancelot Andrewes" (1926).

"John Bramhall" (1927).

"Thoughts After Lambeth" (1931). The 1930 Lambeth Conference has affirmed the Catholicity of the Church of England and strengthened it both within and without.

"Religion and Literature" (1935). "Literary criticism should be completed by criticism from a definite ethical and theological standpoint."

"The *Pensées* of Pascal" (1931). Pascal is a great scientist who defends the Christian faith on the basis of reasons of the heart—more difficult and complex reasons (involving the whole personality) than those of science.

"Baudelaire" (1930). Baudelaire is a poet who raises the imagery of the sordid life of a great metropolis to the first intensity. In his profound capacity for damnation, Baudelaire enters Christianity by the back door.

"Arnold and Pater" (1930). Pater's estheticism is an outgrowth of Arnold's humanism, which subordinates religion to culture.

"Francis Herbert Bradley" (1927).

"Marie Lloyd" (1923). The superiority of Marie Lloyd, a music-hall performer, over other performers is due to "her understanding of the people and sympathy with them."

"Wilkie Collins and Dickens" (1927). Dickens excelled in creating characters of great intensity, and Collins in constructing interesting plots, the essence of melodrama.

"The Humanism of Irving Babbitt" (1928).

"Second Thoughts about Humanism" (1929). "If you remove from the word 'human' all that the belief in the supernatural has given to man, you can view him finally as no more than an extremely clever, adaptable, and mischievous little animal."

"Charles Whibley" (1931). Whibley is a great literary journalist, a master of invective.

"Modern Education and the Classics" (1932): "The first educational task of the communities should be the *preservation* of education within the cloister, uncontaminated by the deluge of barbarism outside."

John Dryden: the Poet, the Dramatist, the Critic. New York, 1932. As a poet and dramatist, Dryden established a "*normal English speech*" for both verse and prose; as a critic, he is a defender of sanity, who assumes that the purpose of poetry is to amuse properly.

Introduction to *The Collected Poems of Harold Monro.* London, 1933). Monro's technique is conventional but his vision is original and personal. "The external world, as it appears in his poetry, is manifestly but the mirror of a darker world within."

*The Use of Poetry and the Use of Criticism: Studies in the
Relation of Criticism to Poetry in England.* London, 1933;
New York, 1933. During the literary periods—from Sidney
to Richards—the concept of the use of poetry is that it
instructs and delights. The Romantics, followed by Arnold
and Richards, conceive of poetry as a substitute for religion.
Criticism asks two major questions, to which it cannot
give satisfactory answers: "what is poetry" and "is this a
good poem?"

After Strange Gods: A Primer of Modern Heresy. London,
1934; New York, 1934. Many contemporary writers—for
example, Thomas Hardy and D. H. Lawrence—are heretical
and morally subversive because they have substituted individualistic morals for an orthodox sensibility (one determined by the Catholic religious tradition).

Elizabethan Essays. London, 1943. Reprinted, except for "John
Marston," from *Selected Essays.*

"Four Elizabethan Dramatists"   "Thomas Middleton"
"Christopher Marlowe"   "Thomas Heywood"
"Shakespeare and the   "Cyril Tourneur"
  Stoicism of Seneca"   "John Ford"
"Hamlet and His Problems"   "Philip Massinger"
"Ben Jonson"   "John Marston"

Introduction to *Selected Poems by Marianne Moore.* New York,
1935. Marianne Moore's poetry realizes the aim of Imagism,
inducing "a peculiar concentration upon something visual"
and setting "in motion an expanding succession of concentric
feelings."

Essays Ancient and Modern. London, 1936; New York, 1936.

Preface. Some of the essays may soon be out of date and will need to be removed from currency. The only unity that the essays possess is that they were written by the same author.

"Lancelot Andrewes."
"John Bramhall."
"Francis Herbert Bradley."
"Baudelaire in Our Time."
"The Humanism of Irving Babbitt."
"Religion and Literature."
"Catholicism and International Order." A Catholic world order "is ultimately the only one which, from any point of view, will work." A Catholic order means a moral order, judged by a transcendent standard, which is far superior to any secular scheme for world harmony.
"The *Pensées* of Pascal."
"Modern Education and the Classics."
"In Memoriam."

The Idea of a Christian Society. London, 1939; New York, 1940. The ideal Christian society is a stratified theocracy, in which the Church determines all matters of dogma and faith. Although the rulers are not required to be Christians, they are required to conform to Christian principles as interpreted by the Church. Dissentients should be held to a minimum.

Notes towards the Definition of Culture. London, 1948; New York, 1949. Culture cannot exist without religion and inequality (in wealth and education). Culture is most likely to flourish in a class society based on tradition. The elite, although admitting those of exceptional talent to its ranks, should be determined by birth.

On Poetry and Poets. New York, 1957.

"The Social Function of Poetry" (1945). The social function of poetry is to enrich the language of a people.

"The Music of Poetry" (1942). The music of poetry is the integration of a "musical pattern of sound and a musical pattern of the secondary meanings of the words."

"What is Minor Poetry?" (1944). A minor poet is one who is not ordinarily read in his entirety, but in two or three representative selections.

"What is a Classic?" (1944). A classic, which is not synonymous with greatness, possesses "maturity of mind, maturity of manners, maturity of language and perfection of the common style," as well as comprehensiveness (a range of feeling applicable to the people of one language) or universality (a range of feeling applicable to all people). Virgil's *Aeneid* is the supreme example of the classic.

"Poetry and Drama" (1951). Dramatic poetry should not be a decoration or embellishment but should justify itself dramatically, achieving an emotional effect that cannot be achieved by prose.

"The Three Voices of Poetry" (1953). The three voices are the poet talking to himself, to an audience, and through a dramatic character. The first two voices are present in nondramatic poetry; all three voices are present in dramatic poetry.

"The Frontiers of Criticism" (1956). Literary criticism is writing which aims to help the reader *"understand and enjoy"* literary works. The best criticism achieves a balance between understanding and enjoyment.

"Virgil and the Christian World" (1951). Virgil's kinship to Christianity exists in his respect for labor, his humility, and his sense of destiny for an ideal Roman Empire; but he lacks the emphasis on love that we find in Dante.

"Sir John Davies" (1926). John Davies, the Elizabethan poet who wrote "Nosce Teipsum" (a discussion of the relationship of the soul to the body) "had that strange gift, so rarely bestowed, for turning thought into feeling."

"Milton I" (1936). Milton is unsatisfactory as a man, a moralist, a theologian, and a political philosopher. In his poetry he sacrifices the visual imagination to the auditory imagination. He has had an unhealthy influence on the poets who follow him; he may "be considered as having done damage to the English language from which it has not wholly recovered."

"Milton II" (1947). Although Milton emphasizes sound at the expense of sight, writing a language that he invented, "poets are sufficiently liberated from Milton's reputation, to approach the study of his work without danger, and with profit to their poetry and to the English language."

"Johnson as Critic and Poet" (1944). Although Johnson's critical theory assumes that poetry should be edifying, he was able, because of the relative stability of his time, to concentrate effectively (particularly in *The Lives of the Poets*) on literature as literature, pointing out merits and defects in imagery and diction. Johnson's "The Vanity of Human Wishes" is great poetry.

"Byron" (1937). Although Byron contributed nothing to the language, *Don Juan* is an excellent poem. In *Don Juan* Byron reveals himself: "the subject matter gave him at last an adequate object for a genuine emotion. The emotion is hatred of hypocrisy."

"Goethe as the Sage" (1955). Eliot says that he had to overcome a "Catholic cast of mind, a Calvinistic heritage, and a Puritanical temperament" in order to appreciate Goethe. He now ranks Goethe with Shakespeare and Dante as "a great European," who possesses permanence, universality, and wisdom (which transcends a particular philosophy).

"Rudyard Kipling" (1941). Kipling is a writer of "great verse," which occasionally contains poetry. Although Kipling is viewed as a popular entertainer, some of his verse and prose is difficult and obscure. His belief in the British Empire is based on his awareness of grandeur and responsibility.

"Yeats" (1940). The poetry of Yeats's maturity reveals a "greater expression of personality"—the "particularity" of personal experience which implies a "general truth." Not only does his poetry give "experience and delight"; it also possesses great "historical importance."

Knowledge and Experience in the Philosophy of F. H. Bradley (London, 1964). This work was originally Eliot's Harvard Ph.D. dissertation in the Department of Philosophy (1916). In the process of knowing, there is a "felt whole in which there are moments of knowledge: the objects are constantly shifting, and new transpositions of objectivity and feeling constantly developing." Knowledge of reality is constructed from "finite centres" (the perspectives of individuals). Our awareness of "the relativity and instrumentality of knowledge . . . impels us toward the Absolute."

APPENDIX I: "The Development of Leibniz' Monadism." Leibniz' "monad is a reincarnation of the form which is the formal cause of Aristotle." But "his monads tend to become atomic centres of force, particular existences. Hence a tendency to psychologism, to maintain that ideas always find their home in particular minds, that they have a psychological as well as a logical existence. Leibniz on this side opened the way for modern idealism."

APPENDIX II: "Leibniz' Monads and Bradley's Finite Centres." There are definite resemblances between the philosophies of Leibniz and Bradley: "(1) complete isolation of monads from each other; (2) sceptical theory of knowledge . . . ; from which follows (3) the indestructibility of the monads; (4) the important doctrine of 'expression.'" But Bradley deals more effectively with the problem of transcendence (the transition from the point of view of one monad to that of others, which constitutes a common vision), although both Bradley and Leibniz fail to face squarely the "ultimate puzzle."

To Criticize the Critic and Other Writings. New York, 1965.

"To Criticize the Critic" (1961). Eliot discusses his work as a poet-critic, dividing it into three historical periods: *The Egoist* (1917-1919); *The Athenaeum* and *The Times Literary Supplement* (the early twenties); and public lectures (the late twenties and after). He emphasizes four points: (1) although there is a continuity in his ideas, his opinions on literature should always be related to the time that they were stated; (2) his generalizations are related to his sensibility—for example, the "objective correlative" to his preference for Shakespeare's later plays, and the "dissociation of sensibility" to his devotion to Donne and the Metaphysicals; (3) his best criticism is that of individual poets who influenced him in the writing of poetry; and (4) his early criticism has been the most influential because it contains a sense of urgency, stemming from the strong convictions of a young poet with a literary cause.

"From Poe to Valéry" (1948). There are three basic reasons for Poe's influence on Baudelaire, Mallarmé, and Valéry (although they did not, of course, all respond in the same way to Poe): (1) their unfamiliarity with English; (2) Poe as the "prototype of *le poète maudit*"; and (3) Poe's theory of the poem as an end in itself, consisting of rhythm and imagery.

"American Literature and the American Language." There are no essential differences between the languages of England and America, but the two countries do have distinct literatures, although we cannot define the particular characteristics of each. Poe, Whitman, and Twain are representatives or "landmarks" of American literature.

"The Aims of Education" (1950). Eliot examines the three aims of education set forth by C. E. M. Joad in *About Education:* (1) preparation for making a living, (2) training in citizenship, and (3) the development of latent powers and faculties. Eliot believes that the three aims are so interrelated that if you concentrate on one you are likely to damage the others. The training for citizenship really means moral training, which involves religion, but no one can say just how religious education should be conducted. A philosophy of education involves a philosophy of man; any educational system will correlate with the philosophy prevailing in the society of which it is a part.

"What Dante Means to Me" (1950). Eliot says that from Jules Laforgue he learned the possibilities of his own idiom of speech; from Baudelaire the "possibility of the juxtaposition of the matter-of-fact and the fantastic"; from Dante the importance, for any poet, of developing the language of his country, of exploring a wide range of emotion, and of being both local and universal.

"The Literature of Politics" (1955). Political parties are of two types, both of which have their dangers: those guided by principle and those guided by practice. There are also two types of conservatives: the men of thought and the men of action, between whom there should be constant contact. Politics becomes ultimately a question of ethics: "What is Man? what are his limitations? what is his misery and what his greatness? and what, finally, his destiny?"

"The Classics and the Man of Letters" (1942). The "maintenance of classical education is essential to the maintenance of the continuity of English Literature."

"Ezra Pound: His Metric and Poetry" (1917).

"Reflections on 'Vers Libre'" (1917). Actually free verse does not exist; all good verse implies some simple meter.

Index

Tourneur, Cyril, 9, 114; personal expression of, 8; emotion and feelings in poetry of, 16
Tradition: as critical standard, 2–3; poet's relation to, 2–3; as order and custom, 3; and orthodoxy, 68–69
"Tradition and the Individual Talent," 4, 97n10, 108; tradition as a standard of literary judgment, 2–3; on emotion and feelings, 16–17, 21, 30
Twain, Mark, 122

Use of Poetry and the Use of Criticism, The, 117; on creative process, 17–18; on biographical element in poetry, 43; on judgment based on meaning, 44, 45

Valéry, Paul, 4, 122
Victorian poetry, 30
Victorian poets, 34
Villon, François, 67
Virgil: in "What is a Classic?" 119
"Virgil and the Christian World," 119
Vivas, Eliseo, 24–28 passim

Warren, Austin, 11. See also Wellek, René

Webster, John, 114
Wellek, René: on impersonal nature of poetry, 11; on problem of belief in poetry, 45–46; on objective correlative, 99n6, 100n8
"What Dante Means to Me," 123
"What is a Classic?" 119
"What is Minor Poetry?" 119
Wheel of Fire, The: Eliot's introduction to, 112–13
Whibley, Charles, 108, 116
Whitman, Walt, 53, 99n6, 122
"Wilkie Collins and Dickens," 116
Willey, Basil: on dissociation of sensibility, 33, 34, 36; The Seventeenth Century Background, 92
Wimsatt, William K., Jr.: on emotion in poetry, 29–30; on "grounds" for emotion, 36; on objective correlative, 100n8,13
Wordsworth, William, 106; joy of creative process, 4; poetry as expression of emotion, 4, 6; role of intellect in creative process, 6; poetic images of, 19
Wyndham, George, 108

Yeats, William Butler, 69–70; personality and impersonality of, 9–10; unorthodox sensibility of, 67
"Yeats," 121

ε